Feb 23, 2015

DIFFICULT PEOPLE

Dealing With Those Who Drive You Crazy

By

Bruce Goettsche and Rick Goettsche

Copyright © 2005 by Bruce Goettsche and Rick Goettsche

Difficult People
by Bruce Goettsche and Rick Goettsche

Printed in the United States of America

ISBN 1-597810-64-9

All rights reserved solely by the author. The author guarantees all contents are original and do not infringe upon the legal rights of any other person or work. No part of this book may be reproduced in any form without the permission of the author. The views expressed in this book are not necessarily those of the publisher.

Unless otherwise indicated, Bible quotations are taken from the HOLY BIBLE, NEW INTERNATIONAL VERSION. Copyright © 1973, 1978, 1984 by International Bible Society. Used by permission of Zondervan. All rights reserved.

www.xulonpress.com

Table of Contents

Preface 7
Introduction 9

1 – The Goal We Pursue 17

2 – The Starting Point For Peace 27

3 – The Most Common Cause of Conflict 37

4 – An Overlooked Option 53

5 – Steps to Conflict Resolution – When You Have Been Hurt 63

6 – Steps to Conflict Resolution – When You Have Hurt Someone 77

7 – Crisis! 89

8 – When It's Time to Part.............................99

9 – Questions 115

10 – A Final Life Principle 127

Preface

We both love the church. It has had a profound and positive impact on our lives and it is a place where we encounter the Lord, find comfort, acceptance and joy. However, we are also concerned about the church. That's why we have written this book. Many churches seem to be fractured by conflict. Instead of people gathered around a church to pray, they often seem to be meeting to complain. The magnetic nature of the love of God's people seems to be losing its power. We hope this book contributes to helping the church change direction.

We decided to write this book as a collaboration, frankly, because we thought it would be fun. The idea of working together as father and son was intriguing. It turned out to be a rewarding experience. We deliberately did not try to indicate who wrote which parts of the book. We felt that would be confusing and unnecessary. We discussed the book and both of us wrote portions and edited the entire document freely. We feel it is a true combination of our hearts and words.

We are grateful to Maggie and Rachel, who have experienced most of the same things we have experienced and they have also tried to apply these same lessons as they have worked with us in ministry. They have been part of the Goettsche team of ministry and we acknowledge that fact with gratitude.

Difficult People

We are grateful to the Union Church of LaHarpe Illinois for their resilient spirit, their consistent love and their simple, yet profound, wisdom. We deeply appreciate the Sunday School class who read these chapters and made many helpful suggestions. We also thank Calvary Baptist Church in Edwardsville, Illinois where Rick has attended and served during his years at Southern Illinois University in Edwardsville, IL. We thank all the different people who have helped us to produce the final work that is before you now.

Thank you to Kathryn Link, for trying to re-teach a couple of guys the English language. Thank you to Greg Walz and Greg Lane for your proofreading, comments, and critiques, they have been helpful. Thank you to the many people in our lives who are displayed here as shining examples of unity. Thank you for bringing glory to the Father by letting your light shine before men. Most importantly, we thank and praise our Lord Jesus Christ, who chose us in Him before the creation of the world to be holy and blameless in His sight (Eph 1:4). We pray that this book will bring healing and head off some future conflicts. May God be pleased to use this book to help us toward the goal of loving each other.

Introduction

One of the first lessons you are given when you go to school is how to get along with others. We are instructed not to touch what belonged to others, don't hit, don't be mean, always hold hands when you are outside and various other guidelines. When these guidelines were violated there were serious repercussions and so very early you learned that "getting along" was important.

The church desperately needs someone to stand up and tell us how to "get along" with each other. If you were to gather any group of people and asked them about their experience in the church, a surprising percentage of those people would share negative memories of hurt and conflict. There are people who carry scars they received from the place that was supposed to be a safe haven, a hospital of grace. There are a growing number of Christians who are aggressive, rather than soft, counterfeit, rather than genuine. Some of these people are hard and abrasive out of self-defense; they don't want to be hurt again.

We had a Pastor who sat in our home in the midst of a community celebration. He had come to say good-bye. Just the previous week the church he served had told him that he "wasn't working out" and his replacement would arrive on Sunday to occupy the parsonage. As he sat in the office in our home, he wept. He was quietly leaving town without so much as a "thank-you" or a "good-bye."

On another occasion, a youth Pastor who had just had a child was told the church was going to "move in a different direction." He was given one week's vacation pay and then was replaced by the son of the Pastor. He and his family were forced to move out of the church owned home and into the basement of a relative. There are times when a church needs to make a change, but it shouldn't be a heartless change.

There are too many stories of Pastors who have been "run out of town" by their congregation after the Pastor had invested years caring for the very people who now turn on him. Pastors know that this kind of thing happens sometimes in the world. They don't expect God's people to act in this manner.

On the other hand there have been many who have been abused by pastoral staff (violating a sacred trust) and found that no one would believe their story. We refer not just to those who have been victims of sexual abuse. There have been leaders who wanted more power and have used many different (and unchristian) means to push some out of the church. Some members of congregations are attacked publicly from the pulpit (certainly an illustration of what is called the 'bully pulpit') or in public meetings. Others are forced out of the church by innuendo and criticism. Some have made mistakes and found that the very congregation that said they would walk with them through the difficult times of life, turned their back in their time of failure when they most needed a friend.

Christians are adopting the militant attitude of the world around them. A Christian publisher sent one of their authors the wrong book and rather than having the mistake met with the compassion and understanding of a follower of Christ, they were told they were "going to Hell." Ironically enough, the author's book was about the Passion of Jesus!

This is not the kind of church that the Lord envisioned

Difficult People

as He commissioned his disciples to "go into all the world and make disciples." Jesus said to His people, "Love one another as I have loved you." Have you ever stopped to ask, what if God turned this around? What if God said, "I will love you in the same way as you love each other." Would such love be pleasant or painful? Would it be enduring or fleeting? Would it give us strength (en-courage us) or take away our strength (dis-courage us)?

As the world looks at the church and at His people today, does it see the Jesus of Scripture? In the early centuries of the church, one of the church Fathers, a man by the name of Tertullian described the nature of the Christian community. Let us paraphrase his words,

> Once a month each person in the church contributes money to the church. Each person only does this if they are able to do so, and want to do so. The money is not used for parties or social events. Instead, the money is used to help the poor and bury poor people, to meet the needs of children and their parents who have little means to help themselves, for shut-ins who are living on a fixed income, to provide for those who have been left homeless, and to help those believers who have been imprisoned or persecuted because of their faith. It is mainly these deeds of love that cause others to notice us. They say, "See how they love one another. These Christ-followers don't seem to care about themselves. They are ready to die for one another and would rather be put to death themselves than watch another suffer. [1]

Be honest, do these words still characterize the Christian community? We're afraid they often do not. Instead, the church is often seen as a place of contention. Churches fight for over many things,

- Style of Worship (contemporary or traditional, expressive or quiet, piano/organ or band; altar calls, no altar calls.)
- Spiritual experience (tongues, no tongues; dramatic conversion, quiet conversion)
- Preferred version of the Bible (King James only, NIV, NASB; literal translation, or dynamic equivalent; gender specific or gender neutral)
- Style of preaching (systematic exposition, or topical)
- Practice of the sacraments (every week communion; believer's baptism, infant baptism; sprinkling or immersion, the value of the ordinances for salvation)
- Theological Preferences (pre-trib, mid-trib, post-trib rapture or no rapture; election and free will; six day creation or gradual creation)
- Personality issues (who gets to "call the shots")
- Financial Issues (which pet project gets funded and which does not)
- Pastoral issues (Pastors people don't like; Pastors who don't do their job, Pastors who insist on controlling everything; Pastors who spend too much money)
- Issues related to church government (should we affiliate with this organization or shouldn't we? Should major decisions be made by congregational vote, by a leadership team, or by the Pastor?)
- Then there are a host of silly issues (the color the church is painted; whether to put pews or chairs in the new sanctuary; who determines how the kitchen is organized?) These issues often become flashpoints that lead to division in the church.

Let's admit a couple of things before we begin our study: Sometimes the church is the most hurtful place in the world.

When we get involved with a community of believers we are looking for people who will share our struggles, encourage our growth, and accompany us on our journey to Heaven. Too often, the church disappoints. Someone has said, "The church is the only army that shoots its own wounded."

Second, we must acknowledge that another person cannot *make* us angry or drive us crazy. We *choose* to respond to their words and actions in this fashion! We could choose to love or to respond with compassion. If we wanted to we could choose to let the words of another simply roll off our backs. When another person irritates us we are choosing to be irritated!

God wants something better for His church and for His people. He wants the world to be drawn toward us rather than repelled by us. He wants His people to reflect Christ rather than distort Him. He wants us to choose love rather than anger. This is the reason we wrote this book.

This book is about Conflict Management. There are many good, detailed, and often-technical books written about the "science" of managing conflict. This book is different because it is written for people looking for simple, Biblical, and practical help to avoid destructive conflict in the church. We want this to be a book that can help the average believer in any circumstance that threatens the peace of Christ's church.

Our experience in the church has been largely positive. We don't have an "ax to grind" as we write. We aren't trying to send any subtle messages or work through some of our past hurts. We love the church and have been blessed by His people.

A number of years ago our congregation received an influx of people who had left a couple of different congregations. One group came from a Pentecostal church; the other came from a traditional Methodist church. When you added this mix of people to the hodgepodge of people who

Difficult People

were already members of the church, it created quite a unique blend of people!

A local Pastor in an act of friendship told Bruce that he should consider moving to another church. When asked, "Why?" the answer given was, "Your congregation is going to blow up with such a mixture of people!" Bruce said he preferred to view the Union Church as a grand experiment in Biblical Christianity. God called a group of people with various personalities and backgrounds to live in unity. To date, this experiment has had a transforming effect on many lives, including our own.

Our belief then, as it is now, is that though a diverse congregation is open to many disagreements, it is also the most Biblical of churches. When people of different backgrounds are made one in Christ, the kingdom is advanced. We believe diversity keeps us honest. It keeps us from drifting into bad theology and narrow-minded practice.

In this short book we will share some of the Biblical principles that have guided our small town church. These simple principles can be used in any setting. We believe the people of God sometimes lack common sense. Often we make things too difficult. God's counsel is not difficult, just ignored. Our challenge is to share and apply what God tells us and try to take His counsel to heart.

This isn't one of those books that will tell you what is wrong with everyone else and what you can do to make others change. This book will lead you to first probe your own heart. We hope to help you evaluate your attitudes as well as your actions. The counsel that follows is counsel we struggle to apply in our own lives. We have discovered that when we pay attention to what God tells us, it is amazing the good advice He gives! God challenges us to become softer people. Soft people encourage peace. Hard people create division.

Please read each chapter prayerfully. Resist the tendency to assign blame and try to diagnose the other guy. Begin by looking at your own heart and the way you relate to others.

We hope you will use this book as a short Bible Study, for a Sunday School class, for leadership development, membership classes, or in a small group. We have added questions at the end of each chapter to facilitate discussion (and hopefully, understanding and love). We hope it will be so easy to read, and so practically helpful that you will want to give copies to your friends. We have deliberately made the book short, hoping this would encourage more people to read the book to the end.

The world desperately needs the church to be the people of God once again. It needs a place where it can find acceptance rather than conflict, joy rather than anger, the truth of the Scriptures rather than accusation and contention from those who look down from ivory towers in judgment. Every child of God needs a place where they can be nurtured. We need a place where we can go to cry, to find strength, to admit our struggles, to stop pretending, to grow, and to worship. This is our pursuit.

Study Questions

1. What conflict situations have you witnessed? What part did you play in the conflict (observer, the one who was offended, the one who was doing the offending, married to someone who was offended etc.)? Write these down, and refer to them as you read this book. Look practically at what could have changed this conflict, be honest, and learn from the problems of the past.
2. What parts of Tertullian's quote are still true of the church?
3. Look at the list of conflict situations listed by the authors. What situations would you add to the list?
4. Discuss some Biblical characters that experienced

conflict? (David and Saul, Cain and Abel, Samson and the Philistines, Moses and Pharaoh, Paul and the Judaizers, Peter and Paul, Euodia and Syntyche). What was the cause of the conflict in each of these examples? What are the positive and negative lessons we can learn from these examples?
5. How do you think non-Christian people view the Christian community? (Contentious or Unified; Loving or Judgmental; A place where they would like to belong or a place that is no different from any other organization: filled with people jockeying for position and power) What reputation do you think your church has in the community?
6. What specific help would you like from this book.

Chapter 1

The Goal We Pursue

Any student of management will tell you the first key to reaching your goal is to clearly define the goal you are pursuing. To state it another way, "the main thing is to keep the main thing, the main thing." It is easy to let secondary issues get in the way of primary issues. It is easy to get distracted.

A car dealer may really enjoy visiting with people. Every time someone comes onto the lot, this guy is the first one out visiting with the people. He learns all about them, counsels them, and befriends them. The people all think he is a great guy. However, if he doesn't sell any cars, he is going to lose his job. The main thing for him is to match the customer with a car that will meet his/her needs. If the car dealer forgets the main thing, he is going to go hungry.

In John chapter 17 Jesus prays for the church. He prayed this prayer on the night He was betrayed and handed over to the religious authorities who intended to kill Him. (We sometimes confuse this prayer with the prayer Jesus prayed in the Garden on Gethsemane. It's a different prayer. John 18:1 sets the chronology, "When he had finished praying, Jesus left with his disciples and crossed the Kidron Valley. On the other side there was an olive grove, and he and his disciples went into it." Jesus and His disciples arrived in the Garden of Gethsemane after this prayer.) Did Jesus announce the prayer? Did He preface the prayer with something? Why is John the only one to record the words? Was he the only one who had a notepad handy?

We don't have the answer to any of these questions. What we do have is this heartfelt prayer in the Gospel of John that gives us a sense of the heart of our Lord for His church. These are important words. Jesus apparently wanted them to be heard.

In verse 11 Jesus prayed for the disciples, "Holy Father, protect them by the power of your name—the name you gave me—so that they may be one as we are one." In verse 20, 21 Jesus adds, "My prayer is not for them alone. I pray also for those who will believe in me through their message, that all of them may be one, Father, just as you are in me and I am in you." In verse 23 Jesus continued, "May they be brought to complete unity to let the world know that you sent me and have loved them even as you have loved me."

The main theme of the prayer is clear. Jesus wants His followers to live in a spirit of unity similar to the three-in-one God. It will take a sharper mind than ours to probe the deep meanings of such a prayer. We know God the Father, Son and Holy Spirit are one. There is no conflict, competition, or irritation among the Trinity. There is only perfect and unwavering oneness. This is the Lord's desire for His people. It is safe to say Jesus wants us to get along with each other.

Jesus knew that a unified church is an effective church. When we keep the peace with each other, the world will take notice and be drawn to the Lord who made us one. When we fight, we appear no different from the rest of the sinful world around us, and people are repelled by the incongruity between what we say and what we do.

Jesus gives us several reasons to pursue peace with our brothers and sisters in Christ.

When we are at Peace With Each Other We Best Reflect the Nature of God

In verse 11 Jesus prayed, "Holy Father, protect them by the power of your name—the name you gave me—so that they may be one as we are one." Jesus declares that one of the key characteristics of the godhead (the relationship of the Father, Son and Holy Spirit) is unity. When we pursue unity, we are seeking the heart or the essence of who God is. When we are one with each other we best reflect God's character.

Do you remember the instruction to husbands in 1 Peter? Husbands are told to "be considerate as you live with your wives, and treat them with respect as the weaker partner and as heirs with you of the gracious gift of life, so that nothing will hinder your prayers. " (1 Peter 3:7) It is that last phrase that interests us, "so that nothing will hinder your prayers." When husbands love, honor and respect their wives they open the door to greater intimacy and union with their Father in Heaven. What is true in marriage is also true in the church. When we experience unity with each other we open the doors of communication with the Father.

Think about it. You know this principle is true from personal experience, don't you? When we are in conflict with another (and it happens more than we like to admit), we find that the joy of the Lord seeps out of our life. When we become filled with envy, resentment, bitterness or an unforgiving heart there is a barrier erected between God and us. We can't seem to connect with the Lord. Instead of peace, we experience churning. Instead of joy, we find turmoil. Our relationship with other people directly affects our relationship with the Lord.

Keeping the Peace With Each Other Increases Our Joy

The next motivation for unity is found in verse 13, "I am coming to you now, but I say these things while I am still in the world, so that they may have the full measure of my joy within them." Why is Jesus praying for unity? He wants us to know and live in His joy.

Look around in a church where conflict is raging. You don't see many smiles and there is little laughter. The music seems lifeless. People huddle in little groups and whisper. There is an awkwardness and tension that even a visitor to the church can detect. Joy is absent. Worship is labored.

Pay attention the next time you are in a room and an adversary of someone in the room arrives. Notice how still and chilled everyone becomes. The tension quickly spreads to those who are aware of the hostilities between the two people. When peace is lacking between us, joy (and love) is also absent. Life is squeezed out of those who are in conflict with each other.

If you are in a love relationship you know that when things are going well in your relationship life is very good. Problems don't seem so great because you know you are not facing them alone. Trying times are overshadowed by the joy of being with the one you love.

It's a different story when there is conflict in the relationship. When a couple is fighting, the poison from the conflict will seep into every other relationship. Co-workers can usually tell when things aren't going well at home. Little things turn into major problems. The feeling of overload comes upon us much more quickly. The fun is drained from our existence.

The story is told that during the American Civil War,

when the rival armies were encamped on the opposite banks of the Potomac River, the Union's band played one of its patriotic tunes, and the Confederate musicians quickly struck up a melody dear to any Southerner's heart. The competition was on.

Then one of the bands started to play "Home, Sweet Home." At this point the barriers came down. The musicians from the other army joined in. Soon voices from both sides of the river could be heard singing, "There is no place like home." Instead of focusing on the points of disagreement, they were finally able to focus on what they held in common.

In a similar way, the church, in spite of its many divisions, is bound together by that one strong link—we are all going home, and to the same home. We are brother and sisters in Christ! We have a common destiny and we should be living in unity.

Peter exhorted the people of God to, "live in harmony with one another; be sympathetic, love as brothers, be compassionate and humble. Do not repay evil with evil or insult with insult, but with blessing, because to this you were called so that you may inherit a blessing." (1 Peter 3:8,9) The blessing of joy will come as we learn to get along with each other.

A Unified Church is the Best Witness to the World

> The third motivation for unity is found in verses 22-23,

> "My prayer is not for them alone. I pray also for those who will believe in me through their message, that all of them may be one, Father, just as you are in me and I am in you. May they also be in us so that the world may believe that you have sent me. I have given them the glory that you gave me,

that they may be one as we are one: I in them and you in me. May they be brought to complete unity to let the world know that you sent me and have loved them even as you have loved me."

We are to be unified so that "the world will know." More people leave a church during a conflict than at any other time. Unfortunately, many who walk away from a church also walk away from the faith. When Christians are in conflict with each other all the talk about love, joy, and peace seem hollow and contrived. People walk away from the Christian faith saying, "If this is Christianity, I want nothing to do with it."

How many people have you heard who said,

- "All Christians do is fight. I don't have to go to church to fight."
- "I left the church because I couldn't take that added tension in my life"
- "Christians are hypocrites. They talk about love but they don't show any of that love in their daily life."
- "I tried to serve in the Church and all I heard were complaints."

Have you ever wondered what makes the difference between a spotlight and a laser beam? How can a medium-power laser burn through steel in a matter of seconds, while the most powerful spotlight can only make it warm? Both may have the same electrical power requirements. The difference is unity.

A laser is best described as a tube filled with gas, with mirrors at each end of this tube. When an electrical current is sent through this gas, there is a powerful reaction. One molecule of gas gets excited. This one molecule grabs another molecule and they move in perfect unity with each other. As each excited molecule reaches out to other molecules the number of molecules moving in unity grows from one or two, to millions. The energy from these molecules moving in unity leave the tube and enter the world and are able to do a powerful work. The difference between a laser and a spotlight is that the laser is focused, and all of its photons (beams of light) are in perfect unison. The photons from a spotlight are not "coherent", they move in every direction. Because of this, they cannot accomplish nearly as much work as a laser can.

When Christians dwell in unity we function like a laser beam. We are focused on serving the Lord, extending His love, and sharing the message of salvation. When we are not unified, we become distracted from our main purposes. Our focus turns to winning an argument rather than honoring the Lord. We begin "competing with other believers and other churches" rather than working to glorify God.

When the church competes rather than cooperates, those outside the church see it as simply another special interest group. We lose our distinctiveness. The reflection of Christ is tarnished and the message of salvation is dismissed as being a meaningless creed recited by those who are part of the "club." People resist the message of salvation because they don't see Jesus making a difference in our lives.

However, when the church *does* live in unity the world takes notice. When the people of God work together, ethnic, racial, economic, and gender barriers disappear. When the unity of the gospel message is pursued, the church is able to work with a supernatural and transforming power. Schools are begun, humanitarian aid is extended, and the discarded people of society are treated as those who are loved by God. When God's people stand in unity the world will see the difference that Jesus makes. The gospel message will have a new credibility. The claim of new life will be evidenced in the people of God. The world will listen.

If keeping the peace was so important to Jesus that he

made it the focus of his final prayer, then the pursuit of unity in the body of Christ should also be important to us. In the chapters ahead we will diagnose the barriers to peace and make some Biblical suggestions for how we can eliminate the barriers so we can become what the Lord wants us to be.

Discussion Questions

1. Give an example of a time when you believe you witnessed the kind of unity that the Lord covets for us. Give an example of a time when you saw the ugly side of the church. What are the differences in these situations? What characterized each kind of situation?
2. Define Christian unity. What is the basis of our unity?
3. What do you think happened to the unity that existed in the early days of the church? (In Paul's letters we sense that unity was already under siege).
4. How might a church in conflict hinder the message of the gospel? In what ways does conflict push people away from the gospel message?
5. Do you think the pursuit of unity can be taken too far? Can we reach a point where our desire to "keep the peace" results in a watered down faith?
6. What is the difference between unity and uniformity?
7. What is the difference between unity and complacency?
8. What is the difference between unity and apathy?
9. What is the difference between unity and compromise?
10. Where do you think your church rates on the Unity Scale?
    - 1- We have no unity. Our church is in the midst of a war.
    - 2- Our unity is very fragile

3- We are unified as a church but it feels like we are at war with believers in other churches.
4- We have a healthy unity and a good working relationship with other churches.
5- We have taken unity to a point where we no longer stand for anything.

Chapter 2

The Starting Point For Peace

If we want to develop unity in the church and in our Christian relationships we need to start the same way Jesus did: by asking God for help. Christians are notorious for neglecting the untapped resource of prayer. We will attend seminars, read books, have countless meetings, hire consultants and try every worldly resource we can think of, before we turn to prayer.

We must change the order of our search. We must begin our quest for supernatural peace by realizing that peace is something only God can produce. It is natural for each of us to seek our own way, to fight for what we want, to push, to shove, and to butt heads. We tend to see every disagreement as a contest to determine who is right and who is wrong. Conflict comes naturally under these circumstances. When someone does something that offends us, we immediately want to fight back . . . looking for peace is not our first response. We must ask God to help us.

Paul told the Ephesians,

> Therefore each of you must put off falsehood and speak truthfully to his neighbor, for we are all members of one body. "In your anger do not sin": Do not let the sun go down while you are still angry, and do not give the devil a foothold. [Ephesians 4:25]

Paul warned Timothy, a young Pastor:

> The Lord's servant must not quarrel; instead, he must be kind to everyone, able to teach, not resentful. Those who oppose him he must gently instruct, in the hope that God will grant them repentance leading them to a knowledge of the truth, and that they will come to their senses and escape from the trap of the devil, who has taken them captive to do his will. [2 Tim. 2:24-26]

When we are at odds with another we are playing into the hands of the Devil. Paul tells us sustained anger gives the Devil a foothold in our lives. He warns us that quarrelling and conflict is the Devil's playground. The Devil is the enemy of unity and peace. Consequently, we must recognize that we are in a spiritual fight and that unity will come only from the Lord.

Be careful here! It is tempting to conclude that anyone who disagrees with you is serving the Devil. It is just as possible that the conflict is the result of the Devil's success in *our* life! There is just as much conflict perpetuated by leaders of the church as there is by those who oppose those leaders. Many people have destroyed their Christian friends and left churches in shambles while feeling they were fighting for the cause of righteousness.

The Devil is committed to bringing division to the

church. If we want to experience the unity of God's grace, we must labor for unity in our praying.

We Should Pray for God to Make us One

The apostle John told us "if we ask anything according to His will, we know that He hears us. And if we know that he hears us, whatever we ask, we know that we have what we have asked for." (1 John 5:14,15) We *know* that it is God's will to pray for unity. The bold promise seems to be: if we sincerely pray for unity, God will answer our prayer.

When was the last time you prayed that God would build and maintain unity in the body of Christ? When you face a conflict, do you pray for God to help you find unity and peace, or do you ask Him to help you "win?" Do you ask God to search your heart, or do you only ask for God to change the "other guy?" How long has it been since you last asked God to bring His supernatural cooperation and peace to the midst of the diversity in your church? Do you pray for the unity of other churches in your community? (It is unfortunate that we tend to see conflict in our sister churches as an "opportunity" to advance our own congregation.)

Here are some practical things to ask for your church

- For leadership to share a common vision
- For those who are recipients of grace to extend grace to others
- For believers to desire to understand as well as to be understood
- For God to root out the remnants of gossip in your church
- For God to help people be truthful and compassionate with each other
- For the church to discern the difference between major and minor issues

- For God to give us an insatiable desire for peace (even though we don't want peace at "any" price.)

We should pray daily for unity because such a prayer will change *our* perspective on our relationships with each other. Think about this practically. If we are praying earnestly for unity, we will be much less likely to provoke a conflict. If we are praying sincerely for unity, then when someone offends us we will more likely look for a way to resolve the offense in love, rather than aggressively strike back. If we are praying for unity, we will be much more aware of the destructive nature of gossip.

Jesus prayed for the unity of the church because He knew that Satan would seek to destroy us by turning us against each other.

We Should Ask God to Help Us Identify the Source of the Problem

Let's be honest with ourselves. Sometimes we don't want to be reconciled! There are times we resist what is necessary to obtain unity because we would rather be mad, complain, gossip and "get even." It's human nature, but it's also sin.

Consider how different our prayers are from the prayer of David in Psalm 139:23,24

> Search *me*, O God, and know *my* heart;
> test *me* and know *my* anxious thoughts.
> See if there is any offensive way in *me*,
> and lead *me* in the way everlasting. [emphasis added]

There are certainly times we must pray for the Lord to stand by our side and vindicate us. However, these times are much less frequent than we think. Before we can pray for

God to defend us, we have to be sure that we are not the cause of the problem.

There have been times when we have gone to the Lord in prayer out of frustration over what someone has said or done. These prayers often have a certain "whine" to them. We tell the Lord how we are being persecuted unjustly. Our unspoken prayer is obvious, "Arise, O Almighty One and Smite My Enemy!" More often than not however, the Lord brings us back to reality with a gnawing question: "Is it possible that the problem is with you?"

A true prayer for unity wants to understand both sides of an issue. Anything less than this is really not a prayer for unity, but a prayer to win! If we are open to the searchlight of God's Spirit, God will ask some important questions. Some of these questions are listed in the next chapter.

There is a wonderful prayer that has been making the rounds on the Internet,

A Different Kind of Prayer

Heavenly Father, help us remember that the person who cut us off in traffic last night is a single mother who worked nine hours that day and is rushing home to cook dinner, help with homework, do the laundry, and spend a few moments with her children.

Help us to remember that the pierced, tattooed, disinterested young man, who can't make change correctly, is a worried 19-year-old college student, balancing his apprehension over final exams with his fear of not getting his student loans for next semester.

Remind us, Lord, that the scary looking bum, begging for money in the same spot every day (who really ought to get a job!) is a slave to addictions that we can only imagine in our worst nightmares.

Help us to remember that the old couple walking annoy-

ingly slow through the store aisles and blocking our shopping progress are savoring this moment, knowing that, based on the biopsy report she got back last week, this will be the last year that they go shopping together.

Heavenly Father, remind us each day that, of all the gifts you give us, the greatest gift is love. It is not enough to share that love with those we hold dear. Open our hearts not just to those who are close to us, but to all humanity. Let us be slow to judge and quick to forgive, show patience, empathy, and love. [Author Unknown]

What makes this prayer so powerful is the perspective of the one who is praying. This person has allowed the Lord to search their heart to give them the perspective needed for love and unity.

Rick had a friend who had just had a fight with his girlfriend. He loved her and was certain this was the girl he wanted to marry, but they had a horrible fight, and both lashed out and said things they shouldn't have said. They parted in anger, and this young man went, as was his custom on this evening, to a gathering of students for a time of worship. After the service, he took Rick aside and said he desperately needed to talk. His ability to worship was compromised by the conflict with his girlfriend. This man had the right approach to the situation. He said, "My girlfriend and I just had a fight. She said some things about me that hurt. What I want from you is not for you to tell me I was right, but to be honest with me, and tell me what my role is in this, what I need to change, and how I should move toward reconciling with her." This man loved his girlfriend enough to look honestly at a conflict situation, not to assign blame, but to bring about understanding, growth, and reconciliation.

This young man understood what it meant to pursue God's peace. The first step to take in any conflict situation is not to marshal support for your position; seek to discredit your opponent, (by calling them stupid, unspiritual, short-sighted); threaten to withdraw from the church, withdraw your resources or flex your muscles through your position or influence. The first step is to pray and ask God to search your own heart and show you where you need to make changes.

Most of us don't like going to the Doctor's office. No one likes to be prodded and poked. We go to the Doctor because we know that early detection saves lives. We don't want to hear that we have the early stages of cancer, but we need to hear these words so we can fight the proper battle. We don't want to hear about our elevated blood pressure, but it is better to hear those words and take corrective action, than to have a heart attack or suffer the effects of a stroke. Sometimes hard words are the most loving words of all.

If you are like us, your best friends are the ones who tell you the truth. While everyone else is trying not to offend you, your best friends will confront you with your wrong-doing. Why? It's because they love you enough to do what is difficult, but best. They would rather risk your friendship than see you move in a direction that will hurt you.

God loves us more than our best friends. As we turn to the Lord in conflict situations we may hear some hard words. They are spoken by God's Spirit not to beat us up but to help us to grow and develop in our faith and in our relationships. Instead of resisting them, we should welcome them as our friends.

We Must Ask God to Give us the Courage to Make the Necessary Changes

Even after we have searched our own heart we still need God's help through prayer. If we have done wrong we need to ask for God's help to admit our wrong and to lead the other person to extend forgiveness.

If we are being attacked unjustly and the problem does lie with the other person, we still need to pray. We must ask God to help us love that person in spite of their actions toward us. We will ask God to help the other person see the wrong they have done so the relationship might be restored. We can pray for an opportunity to talk to the person about the situation (but don't pray such a prayer if you aren't ready for God to provide such an opportunity). It takes courage to make the necessary changes.

The point of all this is simple. We need to learn to pray before we instinctively lash out. We must nurture our relationship with the Lord through quiet times of prayer, reflective Bible study, times of fasting and meditation, and active listening. The only way to change our instinct to strike out at others is to fill our hearts and lives with God's Spirit. He is the only one who can bring the change that's needed for peace.

May we make a suggestion? We suggest you make a prayer for unity a regular part of your daily prayer. One day you can pray for the conflicts that you are aware of by name. On another day, pray for unity among the leadership. On another day pray for unity among the churches in a community. You don't have to ask the same thing every day. Develop a passion for unity by making it a matter of urgency between you and the Lord. The church will regain its influence in the world by God's power and God's power alone.

Discussion Questions

1. Why is the Devil so eager to use conflict? What gains can Satan achieve through conflict among believers?
2. If praying for unity is God's will, why do we so often neglect this responsibility? What tends to be our first instinct in a conflict?
3. Do you agree that our prayers tend to focus more on

"winning" than on being reconciled? What does this tell us about our own attitudes?
4. Why is it necessary to allow God to search our hearts in any conflict situation? Can you think of a time when God changed your attitude? What other questions might God's Spirit raise in your heart in the quiet time of prayer?
5. What would happen in a church where people approached conflict situations in this way? Would disagreement disappear? Would feelings no longer get hurt?
6. If you are going through a time of conflict right now, put down this book and turn to the Lord in prayer. Be specific about the issue and seek God's enlightenment, direction and strength to bring unity in the midst of conflict. Don't hurry this process. Sit silently before the Lord and let His Spirit search your heart.

CHAPTER 3

The Most Common Cause of Conflict

Sometimes the problems in our lives have relatively simple solutions. Unfortunately we sometimes miss these simple solutions because they are too simple. Suppose you have a spending problem. The simple solution is to get rid of all your credit cards so you don't continue to add to your debt. Maybe you have a group of friends who always seem to lead you into trouble. The simple solution would be to get different friends. Maybe you are having trouble understanding the Bible. The simple solution may be to look for a translation of the Bible you do understand.

In this chapter we look at a very simple solution to conflict situations. We believe most of the conflict we have in the church, and with each other, could be quickly diffused if we took a hard look at ourselves and accepted responsibility for our part of the problem.

James, the half-brother of Jesus puts his finger on the

issue quite clearly,

> What causes fights and quarrels among you? Don't they come from your desires that battle within you? You want something but don't get it. You kill and covet, but you cannot have what you want. You quarrel and fight. You do not have, because you do not ask God. When you ask, you do not receive, because you ask with wrong motives, that you may spend what you get on your pleasures. [James 4:1-3]

James doesn't beat around the bush. He asks a question: "Do you want to know why there is so much conflict in our lives and in the church?" Then he answers his question saying, conflict is caused by our own greed, jealousy and pettiness!

Please hear these words. We resist this idea with all of our strength. We want to believe that conflict is always the fault of the other guy. If you ask someone how a conflict began, the most popular answer you will get is, "Well, he/she . . .. " The other guy hurt our feelings, took advantage of a situation, shared a secret, is trying to manipulate us, or failed to do something.

James contends the reason we don't have what we want, and the reason we seem so spiritually lifeless, is because we either don't ask God (we try to bring these things to pass in our own strength) or because we are being selfish. May we put this a little less eloquently? The reason we have so much conflict in our lives is that we keep trying to play God! We want to do things our own way. Conflict is generally caused by our self-centered, competitive and petty human nature. Conflict is the result of sin.

Dallas Willard has written, "Most problems in contemporary churches can be explained by the fact that members have not yet decided to follow Christ" [2] People may have recited a prayer and had an experience, but there is no subsequent transformation in their daily living and attitudes!

When Christians approach conflict the same way the world does, we are bound to fail. The world wants to assign blame; Christians are to seek reconciliation and harmony. The world wants to win every argument; the Christian understands that the first step to unity (God's definition of winning) is humility. The world says, "Avoid accepting responsibility at all costs;" the Lord tells us to, "Confess your sins to one another."

In this chapter we suggest a number of ways we may be the cause of a conflict. This list is certainly not exhaustive, but these are some of the most common causes of conflict. To hear these words and apply them personally will require humility, honesty, and a true desire to follow Christ. It would be good to learn these questions and use them to quickly inventory your own responsibility in every conflict situation.

Am I jumping to conclusions? It's easy for us to jump to a conclusion before we have all the facts. It's so easy we do it all the time. Someone cuts you off in traffic and you assume they are crazy or don't know how to drive. (In truth, they may be in the midst of a crisis that has made them a little careless. It's also possible that they simply misjudged the situation (and let's be honest, it has happened to all of us)). Someone's personality rubs you the wrong way and you conclude they are manipulative, shallow, and arrogant. (However, it's just as possible that your personality is the one with the problem.)

Let's create a situation. A Pastor comes into a board meeting and suggests an ambitious new program for the church. The board responds to the idea with a stunning lack of enthusiasm. In fact, some people at the meeting are obviously against the idea. If we are jumping to conclusions, several things could happen.

Difficult People

The Pastor may be frustrated by the lack of enthusiasm from the Board. Perhaps he heads home to his spouse and proclaims that the board members have no vision or faith. In the Pastor's mind these people are no longer allies but obstacles to overcome. He is convinced they are spiritually shortsighted.

The board members may gather in the parking lot (after the Pastor leaves) and talk about the Pastor's "unrealistic grasp of the financial and personnel demands of his idea." Some may charge that the Pastor has no sense of fiscal responsibility. Others may suggest the Pastor is only interested in the idea because he wants to make a name for himself.

Do you see the problem? When we claim omniscience (being all-knowing) we quickly jump to conclusions. Sometimes our conclusions are correct. Most of the time, they are not. Jumping to conclusions leads to barriers between people. These barriers destroy unity and peace.

In the case of the Pastor and his board it is entirely possible that the Pastor did not consider the financial issues. It is also certainly possible that the board members are not exercising visionary leadership. However, it is just as possible that the Pastor presented things poorly and the Board really doesn't understand the idea. It may be that his timing was wrong for a major new venture. It could be the board resisted the idea simply because it calls for a step of faith they aren't ready to take (the Pastor has been thinking and praying about the idea for much longer than the Board members and the board members may simply need time to warm to the idea). It is likely that if the two groups discussed (rather than argued about) their positions without feeling the need to be defensive, they could refine the proposal so that it was better, stronger, and supported by everyone involved.

Think of a recent conflict in your life or in your church. Is it possible that this conflict came about because people jumped to erroneous conclusions? Do you see how easy this can happen?

- We assume the person who disagrees with our idea is attacking us personally. People who respect us can still disagree with us.
- We assume someone doesn't care about us because he/she didn't come to see us, or our family member, when we were in the hospital. It's just as possible the person didn't know we were in the hospital; was unable to get away because of other commitments; didn't realize the seriousness of the situation; tried to get in touch with you but was unsuccessful; or thought you didn't want visitors.
- We assume someone has no respect for the "history of a given congregation" because they want to make changes in the worship order or change the name of the church. In fact, the person may deeply respect the desire of the church to reach the lost and believes these changes will help the church do so.
- A person failed to carry through on an assignment and you conclude they are unreliable. It is equally possible that the person a) didn't know this was their responsibility (we didn't communicate clearly) or b) they didn't know how to do what they were asked to do (we did not prepare them properly to succeed, so they failed).
- We assume that someone who is "always negative" has a bad attitude when in reality they might be carrying a great burden because of a horrible situation we know nothing about. It is also possible that this person is in a bad mood because we have neglected our responsibility and it has resulted in extra work for this person.

We hope you get the idea. In any conflict situation it is helpful to ask yourself, "Am I drawing conclusions that are premature? Do I have all the facts or do I only *think* I have all the facts?"

Am I making a judgment that is God's alone to make? When someone disagrees with us we often conclude that the person is shortsighted, obstructionist, unspiritual, or a shallow believer. We might say they lack faith and question the validity of their salvation.

Who are we to make such judgments? Only God knows what is in a human heart! Who are we to conclude that someone else is unspiritual because they don't believe as we do? Who are we to decide that our preferences in certain areas (as in styles of worship, construction decisions, vision statements, and programming choices) are the preferences that all truly "spiritual" persons should hold? We are not the standard! The Word of God is the standard!

When people disagree with us it is just as possible that we are wrong in our preferences! It is possible that the voice of disagreement is actually a voice *from* God. The majority is not always right. In fact, as you read the Bible, you see the prophet often stood alone. What if the dissenter is sent by God to keep us from making a terrible mistake?

Why can't a variety of tastes and preferences be acceptable? Different doesn't always mean "better than" or "worse than." Sometimes different just means "different!" Is it really necessary to decide how much water must be used in baptism before we can have fellowship with each other? Do we all have to have the same understanding of the timing of the Lord's return before we can celebrate communion together?

In a conflict situation it is always good to ask, "Am I making a judgment that is not mine to make? Am I guilty of turning my preference into "God's will?"

Am I stoking a fire with my gossip? A minor conflict can turn into a major division when people insist on fanning the flames with gossip. Don't you wonder how many lives have been wounded forever because of the words of their "fellow believers?"

When someone comes to you with a piece of gossip we encourage you to reach for the phone and ask the person being talked about if what you have heard is true. (Also ask the person passing on the information if you can quote them as your source.) It sounds bizarre but it is our experience that in every situation, the person you call will thank you for talking TO them rather than ABOUT them. On occasion what you are told will be true, and then corrective action can be taken.

Too often we are guilty of marshalling support for our viewpoint before we ever talk to the person we disagree with. This is like gathering an army to settle a dispute about a parking spot! The more people who are involved in a conflict the more potentially damaging the conflict will be.

Let us give you one example. Suppose you hear that a spouse of someone you know is "having an affair." This is a serious charge. If you share this information with others instead of talking to the person involved, people will start to "take sides" before you even know what the facts are! People will start putting pressure on the "innocent" spouse to throw their "cheating" spouse out. This *possible* problem is now more difficult to address because too many people are involved.

In any conflict we must ask ourselves, "Am I working to put out a fire of conflict or am I adding fuel to the fire with my gossip and meddling?"

Am I unwilling to forgive? Jesus told us in various parables that we are to forgive others because of what we have been forgiven. Paul challenged us to "Be kind and compassionate to one another, forgiving each other, just as in Christ God forgave you." (Eph. 4:32)

It would be interesting to discover how many conflicts began because one person was unwilling to extend mercy and grace to another. We want people to forgive us. We *need* people to forgive us. We all have bad days. We all say stupid things. We all make choices we wish we could take back. Why is it so difficult for us to extend to others the courtesy and grace we crave and depend on for ourselves?

Let's be honest. Some of the conflict that takes place among believers comes from our desire to punish a person rather than forgive them. Someone hurts our feelings and rather than forgive the offense, we want to make the other person pay for their sin (we'll forgive later!) We tell everyone what the other person did (usually exaggerating the offense to make our position more sympathetic). People take sides and division is soon to follow.

Hebrews 12:15 tells us,

> "See to it that no one misses the grace of God and that no bitter root grows up to cause trouble and defile many."

The writer of Hebrews tells us that an unforgiving heart causes a root of bitterness to grow in us. Just like in plants, the root will push everything else out of the way to feed itself. If we harbor an unforgiving attitude, that root of bitterness will eventually push love, compassion, grace, and mercy out of our hearts and lives. We will be consumed with resentment (which comes from playing an event over and over in our mind), bitterness, and anxiety.

In any conflict situation it is important to ask, "Am I unwilling to show grace and forgiveness to the person who hurt or offended me? What if God treated my sin the same way I am treating this person or situation?"

Am I engaging in a "power play?" There are times when we are responsible for conflict because we consciously or unconsciously want to get "control" from others (shouldn't God's Spirit be the one in control?) We manipulate and create obstacles so that we will be the key player. This often happens in church leadership and any time there is money involved. This desire to "be in charge" has fractured families.

This bullying manipulation creates roadblocks rather than passageways. When we push another person, they often push back. When we talk calmly, we eventually get a calm response in return.

We know of a church where the Pastor had "control issues." One day he simply announced he was removing some elders from their post, not due to sin, but because these elders were "hindering the work of God." He saw their questioning of his ideas as a lack of submission. The church split. The Pastor went to another church several years later and did exactly the same thing! The problem was not the leaders of the church, but the Pastor!

Sometimes a long-time member of a church resents newcomers taking leadership positions. Instead of being grateful for the new ideas, they obstruct new ideas as a way of keeping control. They say things like, "If we add contemporary music to our service, I'll take my tithe and leave!" It happens much more than you would think. The same thing can happen when newcomers to the church want to make wholesale changes. They push, lobby and threaten, hoping to get their way. This is the world's way of accomplishing things, not God's way.

Families are sometimes torn apart because siblings could not agree on how to divide the parent's estate or whether or not to put a parent in a Nursing home. Division can arise because one person pushes their will on the others regarding holiday celebrations, vacation plans, or how to spend the family's disposable income.

To be brutally honest, I (Bruce) have been guilty of trying to "flex my muscle." Once I helped split a church because I pushed a time change for the worship service. On another occasion I met with VBS teachers and chewed them out because the first day hadn't gone well and "they were making me look bad." I was young and wanted to affirm my authority. In truth I was stupid and playing power games. I was the problem in both cases!

On the positive side, a number of years ago the church we have been a part of for years faced a rather daunting building project. The project was well thought out and the congregation was kept informed every step of the way. Not everyone was enthusiastic about taking on a debt to expand the church building. They wanted to know: If the present building had served effectively for all these years, why did we need to add on?

This time, instead of pushing, we waited. We explained, we listened, we prayed, we waited for God's timing. We learned from those who had objections. We considered the fact that the building project may be unnecessary. In the end, we waited seven years. However, in that seven-year period of time we were able to address the reservations of the members and make adjustments to the plan. We allowed the idea to "grow on" those who had not been as deeply a part of the process as the rest of us.

On the day of the congregational vote we knew the congregation would vote to build. Those who were uncomfortable with borrowing money said they would support whatever the congregation decided to do. We built the addition. We paid for it in half the time of the loan, and we lost no members of our church family. We gave God time to cultivate a spirit of unity.

In our instant society we push to have everything right now. That's foolish. We cannot trust our timing. We must trust the timing of the Lord. It is God's church, and we must let Him lead that church. (In fact this could serve as another question for evaluation, "Am I insisting on my timing rather than waiting on the Lord?")

In any conflict situation we need to ask if we are engaged

in manipulative tactics. Are we pushing where we should be trusting?

Am I guilty of some sort of prejudice? Sometimes we conclude a person who doesn't dress very well (by our measurement of style) is a person who has nothing valid to say. Churches are often guilty of not being willing to listen to their young people simply because they are young, or have tattoos or body piercing. We might be rejecting someone because they have a dark past or because of their race. Often older people are dismissed because we think they are "getting senile" (even though we still want them to pay for things!) Sometimes we harbor bitterness toward a person from previous clashes, and no longer listen to them. In each case we are letting our prejudice cause division.

James says, "Listen my dear brothers: Has not God chosen those who are poor in the eyes of the world to be rich in faith and to inherit the kingdom promised to those who love him?" (James 2:5) The principle is simple: God makes a habit of speaking through the unexpected.

If you have spent much time with people you have probably learned about faith from a child. You may have learned about grace from a person with cerebral palsy or contentment from a person who is poor. Maybe you learned about courage and trust from a person afflicted with cancer or generosity from a person who didn't have much but shared it willingly.

In the Bible we learn about true worship from the publican (Luke 18); generosity from the woman with the two coins (Luke 21); genuine conversion from Zacchaeus (Luke 19); and Heaven from the servant, Lazarus (Luke 16). The Son of God was born to teenagers. John the Baptist was the equivalent of today's tongue pierced, tattoo covered Biker. When we dismiss what others have to say because of our prejudice, we are closing our ears to what very well may be the voice of God.

Am I expecting someone to be a mind reader? It is impossible to meet someone's expectations if you don't know what those expectations are. Young married couples get into all kinds of conflict because each person expects the other to know what they are thinking. A person is expected to know that you should always fold the towels a certain way, or that there is only one way to put the toilet paper on the roll. We expect others to know when we should be left alone and when we want company. They should know that money spent over a certain amount should be a mutual decision. We are not mind readers! We can't address the expectations of others if we don't know what those expectations are.

The same thing happens in the church,

- We can't know someone is going through a hard time unless they tell us.
- We can't visit someone who is sick if we don't know they're ill.
- We can't give to a financial need if we aren't made aware of the need
- We can't correct a problem if we don't know the problem exists.

At times we all expect people to read our minds. We expect them to know when we are too busy to just chitchat, running late for an appointment, feeling stressed out by demands, or fighting a nagging headache. When we expect others to know what we have not told them, we are being vastly unfair.

When a husband is angry with his wife he may start snapping at her and treating her in a disrespectful way. As soon as he sees this he needs to ask, "Why am I behaving this way?" The first response is always that SHE is doing something to frustrate him. The second question is more important, "Why am I reacting to what she is doing in this way?" That question, when asked with bold honesty, convicts us of our sin. Sometimes the husband is simply angry that his wife is not doing what he wants her to do, (even though he has not told her of his desires and expectations). This is unfair.

Is it possible the other person is right? We hate to ask this question because if we answer it in the affirmative then we may have to admit that we were wrong! Before we can live in unity with others we will have to come to grips with the fact that we make mistakes. One of the traits that Jesus admonished us to pursue is humility. Humility starts when we realize that we are not perfect and we can learn things from others. Sometimes, others do see a situation more clearly than we do.

There came a time when Bruce had to tell his father that he should not drive any longer. It was a difficult time. Dad loved his independence and loved to drive. In his mind, he was driving as well as he had ever driven. He had lost his objectivity due to Alzheimer's disease. The family had an objectivity that he no longer had. His reaction time was hampered and he was a threat to others when he drove. He had to trust his family and submit to their assessment of his ability.

Sometimes we are too aggressive, too sensitive, and close-minded. Sometimes we do overlook facts. We sometimes draw the wrong conclusion or choose the wrong path. We will never be able to learn from others if we cannot accept the fact that sometimes other people are correct and we are wrong! In addition, if we cannot learn from others, we will severely limit our ability to grow.

Conclusions

We hope you can see how these "sins" can bring havoc in a church or organization. If several people are being as narrow-minded, judgmental and petty as we are, the potential for division is enormous.

Consider how many conflicts begin because of petty issues,

- We felt we were not appreciated
- We believed someone hurt us intentionally
- Our opinions were not embraced by the leaders
- Our preference was not the practice in worship
- Someone sat in our seat (it happens!)
- Nobody called when we were absent
- Our pet project was not embraced
- Someone else was getting more attention than we were

If any of the combatants in a conflict would stop and even consider that the problem may even *partially* be their fault, we would have less conflict. If people would repent of the sin that THEY have committed, much of the conflict would disappear.

If you are facing a conflict situation in your church, home, or business may we make a suggestion? Get out a mirror and ask yourself an honest question. "What part do I play in this conflict?" Your first reaction will be that you have no part in the conflict. We suggest you re-think your answer. There is almost always an attitude that is sinful; conclusions that are inappropriate; and an ego that is getting in the way of solving problems. Instead of pointing fingers at others, work on your own attitudes. Work at becoming a peace facilitator rather than a peace breaker. Try to see other people not as combatants, but as people with feelings, insecurities, needs, and blemishes, just like you.

If we can face conflict situations with humility, we can defuse most of those conflict situations. The attitude you bring to a situation will likely be reflected back to you. If you come in looking for a fight, you are probably going to find one. If you go into a conflict with the desire to promote unity rather than your own agenda you will have much less conflict. If you put God's glory ahead of your own, you will discover peace rather than churning; you will experience oneness rather than division; and people will be drawn to the gospel and the message of salvation rather than being pushed away.

Discussion Questions

1. Why do we so often overlook the real possibility that the source of conflict may be in our own heart?
2. What are some ways to recognize this contentious spirit in us?
3. In this chapter the authors suggest several questions to ask which may show our responsibility for a conflict. Which of these ideas is new to you? Which did you disagree with? What other personal examples can you add to illustrate these principles?
4. Which of these issues do you think is most prominent in the church? Which is most often a barrier with conflict between individual believers?
5. If we asked ourselves these questions first, how do you think these situations could change?
    a. A conflict between a parent and their child over attending a certain activity
    b. A conflict between a husband and wife over the management of money
    c. A conflict between youth group members over which version of the Bible is best
    d. A conflict between a man and woman over an offhand remark ("you shouldn't have said that!" "I was just fooling around.")
    e. A conflict between a long-time member of the church and a newcomer over the order of worship.

Chapter 4

An Overlooked Option

You probably know people who seem to be contentious about everything. They jump on any misspoken word. If you say something happened on a Tuesday, and it really happened on a Wednesday, they make sure you are aware of your mistake. If you recall that something happened 3 years ago, and it was really four, they will call you to task. These folks take great pride in knowing the correct answers to everything. Sometimes, we want to cover the mouth of these people with duct tape just so we can finish a sentence!

There are times to speak and there are times to be silent. There are some issues that should be addressed and others that should simply be overlooked. Some things just aren't worth fighting about.

Have you ever witnessed people who become savages over a ball game? They scream at the umpires, the referees, the opposing players, their own players, their own children and even become hostile with their mate (usually when their mate is telling them to calm down). Their vocabulary degenerates, the veins pop out in their head and neck, and they are an embarrassment to everyone around them. It is foolish to get upset and to destroy our Christian witness because a referee did not make the call we wanted him to make. These games are designed for enjoyment and to teach the skills of discipline, coordination, and teamwork. There is no eternal significance to the final score.

In 1 Corinthians 6 Paul addressed a problem at the church in Corinth. The people were apparently suing each other! We don't know the specifics of the situation. What we do know is that the situation had become an embarrassment to the Kingdom of God. Paul addressed the issue with simple wisdom that will help us face the conflict situations in our lives.

There was a debate going on in a city. The people in the church were divided. Both groups felt the *other* group should be the one to leave the church. Things got so bad that when the Pastor got up to speak, the opposing group talked loudly or sang a hymn, to drown him out. When someone from the other "side" rose to speak, the same thing happened! The people of the church were physically fighting each other. The situation was out of control! Each side believed that if they didn't "win" they would "lose." The conflict became public and the local newspapers reported the details. Eventually the conflict was taken to court. It doesn't matter which side "won." The body of Christ "lost." God was not honored, but dishonored in this debacle.

Paul told the people in Corinth that their constant bickering and lawsuits were a disgrace to God. He asked a simple question that most people would never consider, "Why not rather be wronged?" (v. 7) In other words, why not swallow your loss, overlook the offense and surrender your rights if that is what it will take to keep peace in the church?

Hmmm. Paul seems to encourage us to simply ignore some of the offenses committed against us. This counsel is similar to the admonition of Peter that "love covers a multitude of sins." (1 Peter 4:8) Jesus seemed to counsel the same thing in Matthew 5:34 when he told us, "if someone strikes you on the right cheek, turn to him the other also."

Most of us don't like those verses. If someone attacks us, offends us, or stands in our way, our first reaction is generally NOT to overlook the offense. Our first instinct is to "dig in" and to prepare for battle. We want to draw attention to the offense rather than overlook it. Paul condemns this natural response. But why?

First, we need to overlook some things in order to keep them from becoming bigger than they should be. There was a man in our congregation who passed on some sage advice. A situation had developed in the church and the leaders discussed addressing the issue publicly. This man believed it was a private offense and should be handled privately. His wise words were these, "When a dog relieves himself on the sidewalk, the more you kick it, the more it smells!"

That isn't very spiritual, but it is good advice. There are some issues that should simply be dismissed. To fight about them only turns little things into big things. It doesn't solve anything and only increases the stench!

Is it really necessary to fight over what kind of music is used on Sunday morning? Sure, we have our preferences, but it is just music! Music is wonderful and it is powerful, but it is still just a tool to lead us to the Lord. If we fight about the tool, we make the music the central issue. It's not the central issue! Jesus is.

Do we really need to fight about every little family irritation? If we focus on all the irritations we will no longer be able to see the things that bind us together.

Do we really need to correct every mistake or misspoken word from our friend? The more we do so, the more we discourage and aggravate our friend. Before long, that friend is going to start avoiding us.

We can apply this same principle to: the use of classroom space, redecorating the church, which version of the Bible is put in the pew, whether or not to use projectors in worship, whether the youth should have soda furnished for them or whether they should pay for it themselves, whether people should wear jeans in worship, and hundreds of other issues.

We're not saying we shouldn't talk about these things. We believe we shouldn't fight about these things! The fight will do more harm than good. As brothers and sisters in Christ we should be willing overlook differences in "little things" to maintain the unity of the body of Christ.

Second, we should overlook things because there are times when we will want others to overlook what we do. Let's face it. We all do and say stupid things on occasion. There are times when we are in a bad mood. There are other days when nothing seems to go right. At these times we want people to "cut us some slack." We want people to understand that the sharp words and offensive behavior at these times are aberrations; they are the exception rather than the rule. We yearn for understanding.

What we desire from others is what we should be willing to extend to others. If we want others to overlook the dumb things we sometimes say, we need to overlook the dumb things that other people say to us.

Suppose you are working in your office. You have been laboring over a particular project and are finally "getting a handle" on things, your thoughts are finally beginning to flow. Just then someone bursts into your office and wants to know where the paper towels are stored. Your train of thought has been disrupted. Your insight is lost. Your creativity is stifled. At that moment you are likely to be very frustrated. If you are frustrated enough, your response may be curt. It is not a Christian response. The other person had no way of knowing you were deep in thought. You should apologize and repent.

At that moment your friend or co-worker can take what you said personally or they can realize that they caught you at a bad time and your words came from frustration rather than animosity. They can choose to be angry or choose to overlook the offense. You hope they will overlook your outburst. Now, if you want others to do this for you then it only follows that you should extend the same graciousness.

Third, we should let some things go because it is a situation we can't change. It is foolish and counterproductive to create conflict over something we can't change. When we argue about these things it is frustrating to everyone around.

Here's an example that may strike close to home for you. When a couple is married, it is often the case that an in-law will drive a spouse crazy. They resent the tone of the parent, the way they do things, and the way they feel they are treated. They are frustrated that their spouse isn't "doing something" about these annoyances! More often than not, the other partner responds, "That's just the way they are!"

This is not a "cop-out." Children are well aware of their parents' annoyances. They are also aware of their strengths. They have come to accept the negative traits and cherish the positive ones. We accept our parents for the people they are. We don't make our love conditional on whether or not our parents do what we want them to do all the time. When we fight over our parents it's a foolish fight because we aren't going to disown them (the Bible forbids this) and our parents probably aren't going to change much at this stage of their life. We accept the things we can't change about our physical family, we should do the same for our spiritual family.

You can be frustrated that the Pastor has a lisp but apart from intensive speech therapy (are you willing to pay for that therapy?), it is a situation that cannot be corrected so you need to get over it. You may not like the fact that the air conditioning blows on you during the worship service. If you don't want to move to a new location in the sanctuary, this is really something that can't be changed. You may not like the way a person accompanies the hymns during worship but apart from firing the accompanist (which often will create bigger problems) there is not much accomplished by the complaints.

We could eliminate a great deal of conflict in the church if we stopped complaining about things we can't change. When people get together there will inevitably be different ideas, preferences and personalities, and approaches to the issues of life. If you can't accept that fact, don't complain – stay away from people!

Fourth, we should let some things go because God's reputation is more important than our own. At times we must realize that the unity of the body of Christ is more important than our feelings. What people think about Jesus (as they see Him in the way Christians respond to each other) is much more important than whether or not our "honor" is defended.

A soldier on a battlefield goes out to battle knowing that he may have to give his life in order to defend his country. A doctor goes into medicine knowing there will be late nights and annoying phone calls. A pastor enters ministry knowing he most likely will not be paid what others of his education will be making. Nevertheless, these people make these sacrifices for something that is greater than them. They are willing to give up their rights and comfort so another can benefit. In like manner, we are to be willing to be offended for the benefit of the kingdom.

There are times, frankly, when we should absorb a hurt rather than risk a hurt to the reputation of our Lord. We can't help but wonder if the Lord will someday ask us, "Why did you allow your petty grievances to bring such a stain to my name?" We must desire the Lord's honor more than we seek retribution for a wrong done. The Lord has promised, "Vengeance is mine, I will repay" (Romans 12:19). We must trust him.

Fifth, we should let some things go because it is what grace demands. In John 8 there is the great story of Jesus and the woman caught in adultery. This woman was brought before Jesus by an angry mob that apparently had entrapped her. The man involved in the adultery was nowhere to be found. The woman faced the accusers alone.

The accusers intended to use this woman to undermine the work of Christ. They said to Jesus, "The Law of Moses commanded us to stone such women. Now what do you say?" The accusers figured if Jesus said, "Stone her!" he would get in trouble with the Roman authorities. If He said, "Let her go!" He would deny the Law of Moses and be called a heretic.

Jesus chose a third option, He wrote in the dirt! We don't know what (if anything) he wrote. It may have been various sins the bystanders were guilty of, it could have been the names of some of the accusers, it may have been verses from the Law that mention mercy or Jesus may just have been doodling. We don't know what He wrote, but we do know what happened next. When the people continued to pressure Him, he said, "If any one of you is without sin, let him be the first to throw a stone at her." Then He went back to playing in the dirt.

Checkmate! Jesus had caught the accusers in their own net. If they picked up a stone to throw at the woman, they would have been claiming to be without sin and therefore been guilty of blasphemy and opened themselves to public scrutiny. He had them! One by one they walked away.

The most touching part of the story however is what Jesus said to the woman after everyone else had left. He told her that He did not condemn her. He encouraged her to repent and to leave her life of sin.

Difficult People

Was Jesus being soft on sin? No. He still called her actions sinful. He told her that she needed to repent. However, Jesus knew that this woman (just like each of us) would benefit more from grace than from legalistic justice.

Paul wrote, "Be kind and compassionate to one another, forgiving each other, just as in Christ God forgave you." (Ephesians 4:32) After we have received the grace of God for salvation and new life, how can we refuse to extend similar grace to each other? When we refuse to beat each other up with our sins, we most resemble Jesus.

The Devil understands that the more preoccupied we are with ourselves, the less attentive we will be to the things of God. The Devil wants us to measure everything by our expectations, our needs, and our offenses. God wants us to measure everything by His grace.

Conclusions

It is not easy to overlook an offense (even though we think it should be when we are the offender). We will not be able to overlook the offenses of others until we have fully appreciated the mercy and grace of God toward us.

Think back over this last 24 hours. How many times do you think you offended God's holiness? Think about your thoughts, your actions, and your lack of action. Think about the way you denied Christ with your words, actions, and silence. Think about how many times you did not "love the Lord your God with ALL of your heart, soul, mind and strength." Think about the times you yearned more for the things of the world than the things of Heaven. Does God have reason to be offended at you?

Every day, even as believers, we must realize that we deserve wrath instead of mercy. God's grace, patience, and love should stagger us. The thought that we have been given a place in Heaven, when what we deserve is Hell, should sober us. If we remember what God has overlooked by Christ's blood in our lives, perhaps we will be more willing to overlook the lesser offenses of others toward us.

It is difficult to discern which offenses should be overlooked and which must be addressed. It is easy to say that we should overlook the "little things." Unfortunately, it isn't always so easy to tell the difference between the little things and the big things. Generally, if it happens to us we see it as a big thing. If it happens to another, we believe it is a little thing. We must confront the arrogance in our thinking!

As believers in Christ we have the assurance that God is working in all circumstances. The things that happen to us may simply be laboratory experiences allowed by God so that we can learn how to act with grace and love. It could be that these difficult circumstances are designed by God to teach us to choose His glory rather than our own.

We are not suggesting that we just overlook a case of marital infidelity, a personal public attack, an attack on one of our family members, a case of financial mismanagement, or a whole host of other things. Some things must be confronted. These issues will be addressed in the chapters that follow.

What we are suggesting is that many of the issues that divide us are petty. They are not worth fighting over. We must overlook as many things as we can, and approach the other things with the formula given in Scripture. Moreover, it is the formula for confronting problems that we turn our attention to next.

Discussion Questions

1. Why do you think we so often choose to fight rather than "be wronged?"
2. What are some examples of "little things" that should and could be overlooked?

3. Do you agree that one of the reasons we don't extend grace is because of our own arrogance?
4. Do you believe there are really some situations that cannot be changed?
5. What are the reasons the authors give for covering over another's sin? Restate the reasons in your own words. Which ideas hadn't you thought of before this chapter?
6. What guidelines can we use to tell the difference between a little thing and a big thing?

CHAPTER 5

Steps to Conflict Resolution- When You Have Been Hurt

We have concentrated so far on the preliminary and personal steps in a conflict situation. In this chapter we move to the next step. The Bible recognizes that there are some situations that must be confronted. There are times when we need to make an offense or hurt known to the one who hurt us. There are other times when we need to be made aware of a hurt that we inflicted. Some things cannot be simply overlooked.

We need to confront an issue when it is causes a hurt that hinders our relationship with another. Think about some of the physical injuries we incur. Sometimes we scrape our skin and once we clean out the wound nothing else needs to be done. Some injuries require a bandage. Some injuries require a period of rest. However, there are some injuries that require more focused attention. You may need to have a bone set or a surgical procedure done. Some injuries are life threatening.

In a conflict situation there are some things that aren't a big deal. Some things we can get over in time. These are like the minor injuries of our lives. The majority of injuries and conflict are of this variety. There are however hurts, injuries, and offenses that will not heal on their own. These hurts need to be addressed with the person who hurt you.

There are also church issues that cannot simply be overlooked. Suppose your church has a board member who is upset. The rest of the board has tried to extend grace and mercy to this person. Unfortunately, this "giving in" has only fueled the person's feeling of power. This person now feels like he or she is on a godly crusade to right the wrongs of the board. The problem is becoming increasingly disruptive. The board member lobbies anyone he can find who will listen. Facts are distorted, threats are made, and the temperature of the conflict rises quickly. What do you do?

Jesus gives us some very clear guidelines for the times of conflict. Many conflict situations are never resolved because everyone is waiting for the other party to make the first move. We profess that we would be "more than happy" to be reconciled if the other person would just

>   Admit he was wrong
>   Ask for forgiveness
>   Say he was sorry
>   Make the first move

We need to face a very simple truth: in a conflict situation, each person in the conflict feels that he or she is the one who has been offended! In other words, both parties will do nothing until the other person makes the first move! When neither side makes that first move both parties conclude that the other is acting in a non-Christian manner.

If we listen to and obey the counsel of Jesus, this won't

happen. Jesus told His disciples,

> If your brother sins against you, go and show him his fault, just between the two of you. If he listens to you, you have won your brother over. But if he will not listen, take one or two others along, so that 'every matter may be established by the testimony of two or three witnesses.' If he refuses to listen to them, tell it to the church; and if he refuses to listen even to the church, treat him as you would a pagan or a tax collector. [Matthew 18:15-17]

This is a very familiar passage. In fact it is so familiar that it's easy to miss what it *actually* says because we think we already know what it says. Note that there are several steps listed by Jesus.

The first step is the hardest. **If someone hurts us we are to go and tell the person we are offended or hurt!** Notice, we are not told to wait for the offender to come to us. We are to make the first move! Let's put it another way, when someone hurts you, you have the responsibility to tell the person you have been hurt by his/her words or actions!

Let's go back to our illustration about injuries. Suppose you injure yourself in a sporting activity. You say nothing about the injury even though the pain is intense. You don't want anyone to know you are hurting. When the next contest arrives, you are limited in your ability and performance. When your teammates ask, "Why didn't you get medical attention?" you say, "The Doctor never called me!"

We would think the person was absurd to think he could get medical treatment without alerting medical personnel that there was a problem. Here's the question: When someone offends us, what makes us think the problem will be resolved if we never tell someone that there is a problem?

The natural response is "Why should I have to go to

them? I didn't do anything wrong." Since this person has already hurt us, why would we subject ourselves to further hurt? It's a fair question.

The first answer to that honest question is the strongest; *because it is the Lord's will that we do so.* This is the Lord's command and we must trust that He knows what He is doing. Our job is to be obedient even when we don't understand. If we don't obey the Lord, we should not expect His blessing! However, there are some additional and very practical reasons for the Lord's command.

We must make the first move *because the other person may not know he or she hurt us.* We need to go to those who offended us because it is possible that they do not realize they have offended us. We always assume that another person is aware of the hurt he or she caused us, but often that person has no idea we were hurt by their words or actions. The other person may believe they were joking around and you were enjoying the "good clean fun." Perhaps they meant something entirely different from what you "heard" so they have no idea you were offended.

How often have you seen this obliviousness between a husband and wife or parent and child? They are out with a group of people and one person tells a "funny" story about another, but the person who is the focus of the story is embarrassed and hurt. We give someone a "hard time" but actually are wounding the person with our words. We think it's fine, we're just having fun...but it's not fine.

There are some people who seem to think it is amusing to find the quirks in another and spotlight them for the rest of the world to see. More often than not, the other person doesn't find it amusing at all.

When we are hurt, it's natural for us to feel that the other person should realize what they are saying is hurtful. However, is that realistic? We may be guilty of expecting people to be a mind reader. Perhaps people *should* know they have hurt us, but the only way those people *will* know is if we tell them.

We should make the first move *because the offender may be responding to an offense he or she felt from us.* It just makes sense that since it is possible the other person doesn't realize they have offended you; then you may not realize that you have offended or hurt them.

Let's imagine an example. You are at a church meeting and make a suggestion on how to solve a problem. Another person on the board jumps all over the idea and you feel the words are harsh and demeaning. It's possible that this person is not responding to your idea, but to you personally. Perhaps at a previous meeting this person felt put down by something you said.

It is often a good idea to go to another person about something offensive done to you and begin by saying, "I'm wondering if perhaps I have done something to offend you. The other night at our meeting I felt you were angry and hurtful toward me and I don't understand why I received this response." It is important that we ask this question with a non-aggressive tone. An attack mentality will bring an attack mentality in response. We must go to a person assuming that there is a misunderstanding rather than assuming the attack is personal.

The tone with which we confront a problem is always key to peace and unity. Aggressiveness will breed aggressiveness, loudness will beget loudness, and physical intimidation will eventually get a physical response. We must remain calm because calmness is a prerequisite to understanding in us and for us.

It could be that the other person wants to be reconciled but doesn't know how to begin. Many of us have learned a method of conflict resolution called avoidance. When there is a conflict we avoid talking about it in the hope it will just go away. On minor issues, this sometimes works. On major issues it never works. We avoid the issue but it continues to lurk just beneath the surface of our lives. This cancer continues to eat away at us until we "blow" over something totally unrelated. Unfortunately, for some people, it is the only way they know. They are paralyzed by inaction. If we don't make the first move, the issue will never be resolved.

Finally, we should make the first move *because the body of Christ is at stake*. People draw conclusions about the Lord Jesus from the way they see His followers treating each other. When there is a rift between people, others sense it, our witness is compromised, and God is dishonored. We are to care more for God's honor than our own.

We are to first go privately. There are two dimensions to this command to "show him his fault just between the two of you." Negatively, we are not to talk about the offense to others before we have talked to the person involved. Often this is not the way things are handled. Sinful human nature being what it is, we are much more likely to tell everyone except the offender about the offense.

This isn't fair. It's not fair to draw conclusions before a person has a chance to explain. You wouldn't appreciate it if it happened to you, so you shouldn't do it to others. However, that's easier said than done.

When we make an issue public we involve more people in the conflict and resolution becomes more difficult. We must not confront a person in public unless the offense is a public offense. When the offense is personal the contact should be private.

Too often we have heard about people who lost their temper and railed against a person in a choir practice, board meeting, Sunday School class or worship environment. A public ambush of another person will never lead to resolution of a conflict. When these kinds of public attacks are made, it has the same effect as bringing out large wind fans to quell a forest fire! It is only going to spread the fire of conflict and division.

There is an old story about a man who wanted to teach a poignant lesson to a young student. He told him to go around the large village and place a feather on the front porch of every home. It took most of the day but the student did as the instructor taught him. When the student returned the teacher said, "Tomorrow, I want you to go and retrieve all the feathers you distributed." The student replied, "That will be impossible! The wind will have taken the feathers in hundreds of different directions. I will never find them all. The wise teacher said, "So it is with gossip. It is much easier to deliver the words than to retrieve them later."

The positive side of this command is to go to another in a private place to talk to the person. It is helpful to ask people if you can talk to them in your office, or meet them somewhere for lunch (the social setting sometimes diffuses the situation). The more people who are involved in the conflict, the more complicated things become.

It's important that EVERY time someone comes to us and shares a concern about someone else, we must respond, "Have you talked to him or her about this issue?" If the person has not talked with that person, we must shut down the conversation until he or she has done so.

We are to involve a witness or two if private conversations do not work. It's unfortunate, but sometimes when a person is caught in a sin, instead of confessing that sin, that person will strike out. There is always a risk that a person will take your words, twist them, and use them against you.

We think there are three practical reasons for returning to a person who offended you with a third party. First, it makes you decide whether the issue is truly serious. You aren't going to ask someone else to go with you to confront another if the issue is petty. Second, returning with another person conveys to the offending person that the matter is serious. Sometimes this is all that is necessary for a person to work towards reconciliation. It is easy to shrug off something as a minor issue until a third person is involved. Then, you know this is a serious problem. Third, taking a witness or two with you helps protect you from the other person.

There are some practical guidelines in doing this. First, the other one or two people going with you are not there to help you "win." You are not supposed to be mounting an attack on the person; the other witnesses are there to help gently bring a resolution to the issue. This means that the people you select should share the peacemaker mindset. You should all be sure your intentions are proper before going to see the person again. It is a good idea to spend some time in prayer before the confrontation.

Second, these people should be trustworthy. You must be sure that they would not engage in gossip after the encounter has taken place.

Third, it is important to explain what you have done in your private meeting and help these witnesses understand the situation as you understand it. The witnesses can help us make corrections in our approach to the problem.

If a small group confrontation doesn't work, you are to involve the larger community. Once again, the reason for involving others is to convey the seriousness of the situation, and to stop the problem from going further. This public involvement should start with the church board. The board needs to know what is taking place. This will put them in a position where they can quell talk around the congregation. Their collective wisdom may come up with a way to talk to the offender that will lead to repentance.

The church board is to act in the role of mediator. Their job is not to take sides; it is to find a point of resolution. Most conflict resolution never gets to this point because either the issue is actually petty, or we are not committed enough to the peace process. Sometimes a church board

Difficult People

refuses to act in a Biblical way. It takes courage and commitment to work through conflict.

If the person remains stubbornly unrepentant, the church is to excommunicate the person. These are hard words. We hope a church will never come to this point. Sin is destructive. It destroys people and it destroys churches.

We had a young man on our staff for a short time that had a number of problems. This man's resume looked great and he seemed to have great enthusiasm for his job. Within weeks odd things started to happen. We were told that people saw this prominent member of our staff on a riverboat gambling vessel. The next day, when asked about the comments, he admitted he was on the boat and said he was trying to minister to those who were gambling! He was told he had to make a choice between a gambling boat ministry or ministry in our congregation—he was not going to be able to do both. He said he would abide by the guidelines of the church.

Before long this man was telling everyone around town that he didn't have any food to eat and was having trouble paying his bills. He was getting a good salary for a single man and we wondered if he was gambling again. After some investigation we discovered he had simply changed boats! It was time to involve the Chairman of our Board. He was brought "up to speed" and we agreed that the young man had to resign. At the next board meeting he tendered his resignation saying simply, "things just weren't working out."

Within a week we learned this man was contacting various board members and telling them we had "pushed" him out for "no reason." He was playing the martyr and told everyone he wanted to stay because he loved his job. He told individual board members he was going to ask for a congregational vote of confidence.

We had tried to address this problem privately. It hadn't worked. The Chairman and I both talked to the young man.

71

He claimed he was not talking to anyone about the situation. (We knew he was lying because people were calling us and telling us he had come in to talk to them). We found a letter he had written and confronted him. He quickly left town. In this case, he refused to repent.

The young man was gone but the problem remained. We called a special church board meeting and presented the hard evidence showing that the man had a problem with the truth, with gambling, and perhaps several other things. At this point in the process, we held nothing back. The people needed to know everything we knew. The only way to stop the cancer from spreading was to treat it with the truth. The situation never went beyond the church board and we averted what could have been a major problem.

As we look back on the situation we wish we had involved another person sooner in the process so that we could convey the seriousness of the offense and protect ourselves from the slander.

On another occasion a church leader discovered that a member of its staff was engaged in an extramarital affair. One of the deacons went to the man and talked to him about the situation, he showed from Scripture that he needed to turn from his sin and be reconciled to his wife. The man refused to do so. The Deacon, following the Biblical pattern, went to the Pastor and the Chairman of the Deacon Board, and they all went to this man with essentially the same message. Unfortunately, the man remained unrepentant. At this point, the Pastor consulted the deacons and the church board, and they agreed that action needed to be taken. The Pastor went before the membership of the church, and explained the situation and what had been done already to confront it. He explained the biblical reasons for what had been done and what was about to be done. After much prayer and discussion, the church voted to excommunicate this man. The people of the church were reminded that the purpose of this was not to gossip, but to help bring this man to repentance. The church complied with the decision and removed the man from the church, and did not gossip about the situation. Unfortunately, in this case the man just went down the street to another church where he was welcomed gladly.

The Goal of Confrontation is Reconciliation and Forgiveness. In the verses that immediately follow these instructions in Matthew, Peter asks, "How many times do I have to forgive?" Jesus' response was, "Seventy times seven times." In other words, we should always forgive.

The goal of the confrontation Jesus prescribed is not punishment, but reconciliation. When we confront another person with their offense, and they repent, we are to forgive. In the situation of the man involved in an adulterous relationship, if he ever repents of the sin and comes to the church with this fact, he must be graciously and lovingly restored to the church family. The goal of the action will be accomplished, and a brother will be restored to the church.

Every one of us has hurt someone at one time or another. At times, that hurt was unintentional. At other times, we intentionally (and sinfully) tried to hurt someone. These memories are painful because we know our actions were unbecoming of a child of God. It is hard to admit when we are wrong. When we do so, we pray that the one we wronged will forgive us. We must be willing to extend that same grace to those who wrong us.

Jesus reminds us that the greatest hurt we receive from another is nothing compared to what God has forgiven us in Christ. We are all "recovering sinners." Every one of us lives each day dependent on an undeserved grace. We must remember where we have come from because only then will we be able to extend grace, even to those who have hurt us.

If we follow the Biblical guidelines, our present enemies may actually become our closest friends. In the book of

Proverbs we are told, "Better is open rebuke than hidden love. Wounds from a friend can be trusted." (Pr. 27:5,6) The people who really love you will tell you the truth when you hurt them. These times are never pleasant or easy, but they are often the most important growth times of our life.

If you see someone drowning you have choices: you can ignore the person drowning and declare that it is not your responsibility to rescue others, or you can take the risk and get wet to help another. When someone is caught in the undertow of sin, we also have a choice to make. We can dismiss the person as a loser. This is the easier choice. It involves less turmoil for us. The other alternative is to boldly extend the life preserver of grace. This will often be uncomfortable. It involves some risk. However, it is always the way of the Lord. People who truly care are willing to lovingly confront.

Discussion Questions

1. Why are we so reluctant to tell other people about the hurt we have experienced at their hand?
2. Where do we draw the line between "letting something go" and confrontation? What are some indicators that you must confront? (Can't sleep, can't get past the hurt etc.)
3. What would be a good (and reconciliation seeking) first sentence or two when confronting a person for each of these hurts:
    a. Your feelings were hurt by another's words
    b. You feel someone did not fulfill his/her promise to you
    c. You believe someone was making improper advances to your spouse
    d. You feel someone has treated your child with disrespect

e. You felt overlooked for a leadership position
   f. You believe someone violated your trust.
4. How do you determine the appropriate person to turn to if a one on one meeting bears no fruit?
5. Share a time when you followed these principles. What happened? Was it a positive result or a negative result? Can you think of a time when someone came to you about your behavior? How did you respond? What was the result of the confrontation?

Chapter 6

Steps to Conflict Resolution - When You Have Hurt Someone

In the last chapter we looked at what we are supposed to do if someone hurts us. Sometimes, however we are not the one offended, we are the offender. We did something wrong that hurt another (whether they are aware of it or not). In this chapter we ask the question: What is our responsibility if we know we hurt someone? As always, the place to start is to see what Jesus says.

> Therefore, if you are offering your gift at the altar and there remember that your brother has something against you, leave your gift there in front of the altar. First go and be reconciled to your brother; then come and offer your gift. "Settle matters quickly with your adversary who is taking you to

court. Do it while you are still with him on the way, or he may hand you over to the judge, and the judge may hand you over to the officer, and you may be thrown into prison. [Matthew 5:23-25]

Isn't that interesting? Once again, WE are to make the first move. In other words, in any conflict situation we are always supposed to be the first to take action. We NEVER can use the excuse, "I'm waiting for the other person to say they are sorry or to tell me that I hurt them." We have the responsibility to pursue reconciliation.

Our Lord set things up this way because He knows human nature. He knows our tendency to dwell on what the other guy is supposed to do while neglecting our responsibility. Although it is true that when a brother or sister in Christ hurts us or is hurt by us he or she is supposed to come to us and tell us. However, it is more important that we realize and act on the fact that when we know that we have hurt someone or been offended by someone we are to go directly to them. We are not to stop and share our struggles with others, we are to go and be reconciled with our brother or sister. If we are living obediently we should meet each other on the road!

The intent of the passage is clear: anytime there is a problem *we* are to take initiative in seeking to promote the unity and growth of the church. We must lead by example.

When We Have Done Wrong And Go to Another

When we are the offender there are several things we will need to do in order to be reconciled. **First, we must identify our transgression**. It's not enough to act like the little child who simply says, "sorry!" to keep from being punished by their parents. We must be specific about what we did.

If you offended someone with your words, you need to say; "I know I hurt you when I told others what you told me in private. I am sorry for violating your confidence. I feel awful. Your friendship means more to me than I made it seem. Please forgive me."

If you offended someone with your actions you need to be just as clear: "When I took credit for your idea I realize I was stealing from you. I am sorry. I will make sure you get the credit for the idea. Please forgive me for being so selfish."

Is this hard to do? You had better believe it's hard to do. We would much rather cover our sins than admit them. However, we must be specific. When we are specific, we show the other person that we are really aware of the nature of our offense. We show that we understand how and why we hurt the other person.

Once we have admitted our sin **we also need to seek to make restitution when possible**. True repentance makes every effort to make right the wrong that was committed. If you stole from someone you must be willing to replace what was stolen. If you gossiped about someone you must be willing to confess you had the information wrong. If your sin involved a group of people, you need to make it right with the group. If we are not willing to make restitution we are not really trying to restore the relationship, we are just trying to get ourselves off the hook!

Ken Sande has an excellent piece called "The Seven A's of Confession"[3]

> Address everyone involved (All those whom you affected)
> Avoid *if, but,* and *maybe* (Do not try to excuse your wrongs)
> Admit specifically (Both attitudes and actions)
> Acknowledge the hurt (Express sorrow for hurting someone)

Accept the consequences (Such as making restitution)
Alter your behavior (Change your attitudes and actions)
Ask for forgiveness

When Someone Tells You They Were Wronged By Something You Did

When someone tells you that you offended or hurt him or her we must remember it is difficult to go to someone to apologize. It's even more difficult when someone comes to you and tells you that you hurt them. This is a difficult situation because it often catches us by surprise. Our first reaction is to defend ourselves and place the blame on the other person. In this case, our first reaction is not the right reaction. There are several things to keep in mind when someone tells us we have offended him.

First, we must listen. To put it negatively, don't defend yourself, don't explain your actions, and don't counterattack. We need to understand how the person is hurt. This is different than merely listening for what you did wrong. We must work to understand how our actions affected our brother or sister in Christ. We must listen to the facts and seek to understand how those facts hurt the person. Part of the listening process may include asking questions to truly help you to understand the effects of your actions. You might ask, "What did I do that hurt you?" or "How did you interpret what I said/did?" "How did that make you feel?" These questions can help us understand the true nature of the hurt. You can't make something right if you don't know what's wrong.

Second, we must ask for forgiveness. Asking for forgiveness is more than saying, "I'm sorry." When we ask someone to forgive us we must clearly state the problem and

Difficult People

the result (so we show we understand); explain any circumstances that may have caused us to act the way we did (not as an excuse, but as a way of deepening understanding) and then ask our brother or sister to forgive us. Let's try to illustrate this principle.

Fred comes to you and asks if he can talk to your privately. In private, he tells you that he has a problem with the fact that he was not asked to continue as a Sunday School teacher. He explains that he always felt he had a gift with the children. It was his way of serving the church and he doesn't understand why he was removed.

In listening to Fred you realize that here is a man who feels cast aside and rejected. You know that this was not the intention. In fact, it is possible that Fred was replaced because you knew he was in the process of taking cancer treatments; or maybe you felt he was over committed and could use some time off from his Sunday School responsibilities; or maybe you didn't think Fred was doing a good job. It doesn't matter what the mitigating circumstances were at this point. The first thing you need to do is let Fred know that you really do understand his hurt.

Second, you will try to rebuild the relationship by asking Fred to forgive you. You might say, "Fred, I am so very sorry. I didn't realize what joy and satisfaction you derived from leading Sunday School. I badly misjudged the situation. I was concerned for your stamina (or I felt we weren't using you in the most effective position). I didn't realize that your ministry with the children was the thing that helped you keep balance in your life. I am sorry that I've hurt you. Please forgive me. Is there some way we can make this situation right?"

You have communicated to Fred: 1) that you understand his hurt. 2) You are taking responsibility for your offense. 3) You value him. 4) You want to resolve the situation.

At this point the issue is not how to defend you. We must

listen and accept the responsibility that is ours, and work to make things right.

I [Bruce] had an experience once when someone came to my office to explain an offense that I had committed. I admittedly had been upset at a situation that had taken place (and did not talk to the person about it thinking it was something I could just overlook). Because of my frustration, I acted childishly and showed my displeasure in my actions. This was offensive (rightly) to the person who had worked hard to plan this event.

This person followed the Biblical mandate. She came into my office (confronting your Pastor is never easy) and asked to share a list of things that she had found hurtful. She was specific and accurate in most of what she said. I was guilty on almost every count. I realized that I was being selfish and never considered what this meant to her. I explained my frustration and asked forgiveness for the horrible way I behaved. The issue was settled between the two of us. I gained a new respect for her and I hope our relationship is stronger because of the way things were handled. I learned that in the future, when I have a problem with what is happening I need to communicate that fact before the situation becomes a problem.

However, what if the offense is perceived and not actual? What if a person has misunderstood something that you said? What if they misinterpreted an action and took something personally that was not personal? We've done this to others and it will happen to us. In this case we must affirm our regard for our brother or sister in Christ, explain the situation, and apologize for anything that you did that may have given the wrong impression.

What if the hurt *was* intentional? There are times when we mean to wound another. It happens in marriage, in the family, in the workplace, and in the church. There are times when we get angry and "go for the jugular." We attack a person where we know they will be vulnerable and seek to hurt them deeply.

In these situations we *must* take responsibility for our behavior. We have to admit that we wanted to hurt the other person. We can try to explain why we tried to hurt them but we must not use the explanation as an excuse. There is no excuse for striking out at another. We must ask for forgiveness, make any restitution necessary, and work to restore the relationship.

We value those people in our lives that care enough about us to confront us when we have done something wrong. We never enjoy having our errors exposed but we know if these people wanted to hurt us they would talk *about us* rather than *to us*. We need to listen to these friends and brothers. They are among the most valuable people in our lives. Whenever we work through a difficulty our friendship gets stronger.

Restoring Relationships

The first step toward restoring any relationship is a willingness to forgive. If a person has come to us seeking to resolve a conflict, then we are only creating a new conflict situation if we do not forgive him and try to restore the relationship. This means that we must be gracious in the way that we treat someone who comes to us. Revenge is human but counterproductive. We must fight the urge to deepen the hurt by striking back. We should not try to make the person feel even worse, but it is important for them to understand your hurt. Express the pain you felt from that hurt. Focus on the fact that there is now a burden that has been lifted from both of your shoulders. The healing process can now begin.

True forgiveness involves letting the matter go. It means we no longer think about the issue, talk about the issue or use it against the other person in the future. True forgiveness results in a restored relationship.

If you are the one who was hurt, we suggest that before you part company, you extend a hand or, if appropriate, give the other person a hug. Physical touch can often express more to a person than any words can. That touch lets them feel that you have indeed forgiven them.

If you were the offender, before you part company, reiterate your sorrow for hurting your brother and your gratitude for the fact that they came to you or forgave you. You also need to extend a hand or ask if you may give the other person a hug. This will show that you really do want the relationship to be right.

After the initial encounter is over, there is often an awkwardness that occurs between the people involved. We can help that disappear and help the offender (or offended) know that the relationship is restored in a number of ways:

- Smile at the person when you see him/her next
- Say hello and strike up a conversation
- Extend your hand
- Approach the individual and talk to him/her, don't wait for the person to come to you.
- Try to keep in touch in some way, don't just leave things the way they are.

Reconciliation takes work. The Bible is clear that a Christian person will work hard not only at confronting a problem but also at restoring the broken relationship.

Conclusions

Many of us don't happen to be naturally aggressive persons when it comes to conflict. We don't like taking the initiative when we have done something wrong or have been offended. We'd rather ignore the situation and hope it goes away. If we have learned anything in this study it is that

God's way really is the best way. If we don't confront a problem early, it tends to gnaw at us and grow in size and proportion. If we don't confess a sin quickly the chasm between us grows greater.

There is a real good chance there is someone in your life right now you need to go talk to. You either need to apologize or explain your hurt. It could be that this is something you have needed to do for years. Maybe you feel like it has been too long. Mark these words: It is never too late to do what is right.

There have been a few times in our lives when we have written letters to people from the past to ask for forgiveness for foolish and sinful behavior. It was always difficult but those letters were always received graciously.

We believe most people don't like being estranged from us any more than we like being estranged from them. We also think most people don't know how to make the first move. Somebody has to take the first step, why shouldn't that someone be you? We encourage you to,

- Make that visit
- Pick up the phone
- Write that letter
- Extend a hand
- Say the first "hello"

Begin in your own family. Perhaps there is a sibling, parent, child, aunt or uncle with whom you need to work on building a bridge. Show your love by working hard to eliminate the wall between you. Demonstrate your love for Christ by being obedient in this area of your life.

Next, move to your church family, work contacts, friends and neighbors. Take that first step toward the unity that God wants for His family of faith. Make an appointment with the Pastor, board member or other member of the congregation where you know things are strained. Ask a co-worker if they have a moment to talk after work. Call up a friend and ask if you can meet them for a cup of coffee. Find out what the problem is and work through it. Do it for the Savior's sake.

You are going to find that some people didn't realize that there was a problem and you will quickly be reconciled. There will be others who will be grateful for the opportunity to talk through a painful situation. It may take patience and lots of humility on your part, but the work can be done. Of course, there may also be that person who refuses to acknowledge a problem and refuses to accept responsibility. In these cases we must follow the guidelines from Matthew 18.

Paul told us that we are to "make every effort to do what leads to peace and mutual edification." (Romans 14:19). In Ephesians we are told to "make every effort to keep the unity of the Spirit through the bond of peace." (Ephesians 4:3). In addition, the author of the book of Hebrews wrote, "Make every effort to live in peace with all men." (Hebrews 12:14). Do you see the common thread? We are to make EVERY EFFORT. That means we need to need to start by making SOME effort. It is not enough to sit and complain. We have an obligation to pursue peace and unity. We have the responsibility to protect the unity of the family of God. It won't be easy, but it will be worth it.

Discussion Questions

1. Why is it so hard to go to another person and admit we were wrong?
2. When have you experienced a time where you and another person were in a conflict? How would the principles laid out in this chapter have changed the outcome of that conflict?
3. When you have done something wrong, what helps

you to feel forgiven?
4. When you have been offended, what makes you believe a person is sincerely sorry?
5. What practical ideas do you have for ways to continue the mending process after an offense?
6. What kinds of people do you find hardest to confront? Why?
7. What situations are there in your own life where you need to be reconciled? What do you need to do to start along that road?
8. Are there times when the best course for getting along with someone might be to keep your distance?

Chapter 7

Crisis!

Most of what we have written in this book is designed to prevent conflict. We want to help the body of Christ grow to maturity in our dealings with each other.

With that said, it is possible that the conflict that caused you to pick up this book is already out of control. Sides have been drawn. Things have been said. The verbal bombing has already started. Perhaps a church has split, a family has divided, friends are no longer speaking to each other or a work place has become a war zone. Whatever the source of the conflict, things have gotten out of control. In this chapter we want to give you some practical guidelines for putting out these raging fires. We can only give you an introduction. There are several good books on managing full-scale conflict. [4]

Take Action

When the fires of conflict rage, it is essential we take

decisive action. Ignoring the conflict is not going to make the situation better, no matter how long you wait. The longer you wait to address the issue; the more damage may be done. People who are upset talk to other people and get them upset too. This has a snowball effect.

If your conflict is church related, get the church board together to talk frankly and honestly about what is taking place. It is important to get all the facts and understand the various sides of the issue. The goal here is not to determine the winner and the loser in the conflict, the goal is to bring reconciliation and preserve the unity of the church.

If possible, we suggest you bring the various parties together so that conversation can take place face to face. It is important that the tone of the meetings be one of love and come from a desire to address these issues as brothers and sisters in Christ. Any attempts to ambush one group or another in a meeting such as this will only serve as a powerful wind that will spread the fire.

If there are many people involved, it is important that you bring together the most rational people on the various sides of the issue. Some people don't desire understanding; they want "victory." These people are trouble to any peace process. They will come to a meeting to make demands and blast away at their "adversaries." They may be decent people, but in this setting, they are working for the Devil. You need people at the table who want to resolve things in a Christian way.

Action is necessary but it must be the right action. Any attempt to dismiss a problem or to bully someone into submission is not going to be effective. Public rebukes (whether from the pulpit or in some other public venue like a newspaper), vitriolic letters, and ultimatums only make matters worse because it is an unfair fight. Heartfelt prayer must precede any action we take. We must confront our own responsibility in the conflict and seek the Lord for the right attitude.

It may be a situation where your church will have to exercise church discipline. Some of the troublemakers may need to be confronted and if resolution cannot be gained, asked to leave. In any case of church discipline, however, it is always important to remember that this is not to be a quick way of getting rid of the problem. Church discipline is to be used only after the steps to reconciliation (talking to the person one on one; talking to the person with a witness; bringing the person before the church board.) This is a last step, not a first one. It is a very difficult thing to do. Sometimes, like surgery to remove cancer from a body, it is necessary.

If a personal problem is between two believers it is right to ask the church to serve as an arbiter. The people who serve in such capacity must be able to look at the situation objectively with the purpose of bringing healing and understanding.

Pray Fervently

When there is conflict between believers, a spiritual battle is taking place. Satan will seek to use this conflict to divide the body of Christ. He will try to use this time to diminish our witness and to separate friends. Make no mistake; this battle will be won only on our knees.

There are several things to pray for:

- Ask God to lead you to the right attitude
- Ask God to bind the Devil as he seeks to work on both sides of an issue
- Ask God to soften rather than harden *our* hearts
- Ask God to give the leaders courage, wisdom and a heart of mercy and compassion.
- Ask God to glorify His name by the way the conflict is handled. Conflict is going to happen. How the conflict is dealt with will speak volumes about our faith

and Christlikeness.

Examine Yourself Thoroughly

As we have mentioned throughout this book, the first step to peace is always a look upward and then inward. We must begin with ourselves. We need to ask ourselves a series of questions and must answer them prayerfully, humbly and honestly.

If you are a Pastor embroiled in controversy, here are some important questions to ask.

1. Is there some sin that I should acknowledge? If we come into a meeting with a spirit of repentance and humility, others will be more likely to adopt that same attitude.
2. Am I responsible for this controversy because I have failed to teach Biblically or love compassionately? Again, it's time to confess and seek forgiveness.
3. Have I brought on this conflict by making my program or vision more important than the people of the church? Am I trying to lead the church rather than follow the Spirit's leading for the church? Am I so focused on being successful that I have forgotten that my definition of success may not be the same as that of the Lord?
4. Am I pushing the congregation to make a change it is not ready to make? (For example, there are always those Pastors who come into a church and make wholesale changes before taking time to understand and appreciate the methods and traditions of their congregations. This makes a congregations feel like it has been spiritually "raped.") It may be time to slow the timetable of change to allow others to adjust to what is happening.

5. Am I not doing my job (visiting the sick, ministering to the troubled, leading in worship, preparing diligently for teaching times)? Let's admit that the requirements of the job are often more than what one person can reasonably be expected to do. However, it is better to be honest about our inability and ask for help rather than claim the criticism is not true. If we're not getting out to see those who need to be seen, let's be honest and ask for some help in determining what visits need to be made. If we don't have time for preparation, let's admit that and ask for guidance on how to get that time.
6. Is this conflict a sign that it is time to leave?

If you are a church member (not a Pastor) there are some questions for you to answer also. These must be asked with as much honesty as you can muster. They are hard questions but necessary.

1. Do I have a Biblical reason for my position? Am I arguing for a Biblical principle or a personal principle?
2. Am I using the Biblical text fairly? Am I quoting it within the context of its passage and within the context of the entirety of Scripture? (You can prove anything from the Bible if you don't care about the context; or the real meaning).
3. Have I gone personally to those with whom I have a disagreement?
4. Has my demeanor been that of Christ or the Devil?
5. Am I blowing the situation out of proportion by attributing false motives to the one(s) I disagree with? Am I taking everything too personally? What is the *real* issue?
6. Am I attacking people instead of what people believe/do?

7. Am I trying to wrestle control from someone or am I honestly seeking to be faithful to the Lord's will? (Almost every church conflict is a control issue of some kind.)

If your conflict is with a difficult person outside of the church, you have some tough questions to ask yourself,

1. Am I overreacting?
2. Am I deepening the crisis or diffusing the crisis with my attitude/response?
3. Have I truly asked God to give me understanding or am I only asking Him to help me win?
4. Is this a personal issue or a theological issue? (Don't answer too quickly here!)
5. What would Jesus do in this situation?
6. Is the price of "winning" worth the cost of our friendship or family?

Be careful please! It is not your job to tell the other person in a conflict that they should use these questions to evaluate their own heart (unless you are going to both ask the questions of yourselves and discuss what you learned). Your job is to examine your own heart. In any conflict situation, if one person changes, the other person must change in some way also because the dynamics of the relationship have changed.

Any attempt to tell another how to "correct their attitude" will be seen as condescending and will make matters worse rather than better.

Define The Issue Precisely

Much of the time people are angry at each other but don't know why they are angry. We are told they are angry because they "had their feelings hurt." However, how did they have their feelings hurt? Was it something someone did or was it because of something someone didn't do? Why did this act or omission hurt their feelings?

At times, you may hear someone say, "The church has lost its Biblical root." What does that mean? In what way has it drifted from the Bible? Has the church truly drifted from Scripture or has it drifted from tradition (the way we have always done things)? There is a huge difference between these two things.

Before you can put out a fire, you have to know where it is. Fire departments now use rescue cams. These cameras help firemen to see "heat" in a building. This helps them spot bodies in the dense smoke. The cameras also help fireman locate hot spots in a building so they can address lingering parts of a fire.

It's too bad there isn't a rescue cam to use for the fires of interpersonal conflict. A church or individual must work hard to discover where the heat is. They need to find the "real" issues behind the conflict. Once these issues are discovered and everyone agrees that these are the issues, you have a chance to make some progress toward agreement.

Conflict is often messy and very difficult to resolve. However, if you are willing to work hard, be honest with yourself, define the issues, and trust in God's strength . . . conflict can lead to growth. A mature church will work through their disagreements. It has to. Mature believers will not be content to simply write someone off. They will work hard to build bridges instead of walls.

Consider marriage conflict. The problem in many marriages is that a husband and wife are angry and both people think they know what the fight is about. Often each person feels they are fighting about something entirely different. Assumption is deadly in conflict. We must ask for clarification so we can understand where the fire is located.

Some Simple Guidelines

Whatever the crisis there are some simple principles that can help us. *First, a public crisis should be dealt with publicly.* When an entire congregation is involved in a conflict it will also need to be involved in the resolution of that conflict. If the congregation is not involved, pockets of bitterness and misinformation will continue to plague the family, church, or organization.

There are many situations when the best thing that could happen would be for the entire church to be sent to the Fellowship Hall, lock the doors, and let them work things out. It is important that everyone hear all the same information (because it will not be relayed accurately).

Obviously, if a problem can be addressed early when only a few people are involved, that situation is the best situation. However, once things have gone "public", the issue must now be resolved publicly.

The second principle has been alluded to already; *more accurate information is better than less information that relies on supposition to fill in the blanks.* It is obvious that a church must never share privileged information. However, in the case of privileged information (something that was told to the Pastor in confidence) it is important to share the fact that the information is privileged. That may be frustrating to people but it also lets them know that their privileged information will not be shared either.

At the same time, the more accurate information that can be shared, the better. It is good to report exactly when and what was said. It is good to outline the steps that led to the present crisis. If everyone has the same information it will be much easier to come to a place of understanding and agreement.

Third, *if there is no objective person available to moderate a discussion every effort should be made to find one.*

Sometimes, the people involved in a controversy will have lost their objectivity. An objective moderator is necessary to help people reach an agreement. This may be a person from the church, an area minister, a denominational specialist or a professional Christian mediator or a mutual friend. The more serious the conflict, the more skilled a moderator you will need.

Fourth, *God's Glory should be the central goal.* We need to remind ourselves repeatedly that a conflict between Christians diminishes God's glory! Periodically we will need to repeat that resolving the conflict is "not about me." It is a Christian matter, rather than a personal matter. God's honor is at stake!

Even the worst of conflicts can be beneficial to the church or relationship if it is handled correctly. Even the most trivial of conflicts can deeply wound a church, friendship, or family if it is handled poorly. In any conflict there must be someone courageous enough to humbly call the parties to the table of reconciliation for the sake of the body.

It's our hope that you never face a crisis of this magnitude in your church or in your family. If you and the leaders of your church follow the principles in the first several chapters you will be spared most if not all of these conflicts. The more we attack the worse things get. The more we listen and pray the better things will become.

Discussion Questions

1. What happens to the reasoning ability of people in times of conflict? Why is this so? What can be done to counteract this tendency?
2. What does Satan have to gain from conflict situations?
3. List some additional reasons that people have given for conflict in a church. Try to further define what these reasons mean?

4. List some examples of interpersonal conflict that might have been lessened if people had listened to each other.
5. Can you relate any times when a church exercised church discipline or removed someone from membership? Why is church discipline such a difficult thing for churches to do? (Consider: what sins should be addressed? How do you begin after a long history of no church discipline? What is gained if the person is just going to start attending the church down the street? How involved should a church become in the personal conflicts of its members?)

Chapter 8

When It's Time To Part

So far in our study our aim has been to pursue the unity of the Spirit through the bond of peace. (Ephesians 4:3) We have suggested heartfelt prayer, doing a personal inventory, working on our own maturity, overlooking faults, and following the Biblical guidelines for confrontation. We believe these common sense approaches to conflict situations will bring reconciliation to most conflict in the body of Christ. However, there are some conflict situations that may only be resolved by parting company.

The Apostle Paul wrote," If it is possible, as far as it depends on you, live at peace with everyone." (Romans 12:18) The words, "if at all possible" indicate that apparently, even after you have made every effort to maintain unity, peace is not always possible. Jesus told His disciples that after visiting some cities they were to shake the dust off their feet and go on. In the book of Titus, Paul advised his friend, "Warn a divisive person once, then warn them a second time, then have nothing more to do with them. You can be sure that such a person is warped and sinful, he is self-condemned"(3:10). There are times we must part company.

This is a dangerous chapter because human nature being what it is, we all feel like we are standing on principle in every conflict we are involved in. No one starts out believing that their conflict is an issue that should simply be overlooked out of love for their opponent, the church, and the Lord. No one gets involved in a conflict thinking, "I want to have a tantrum." The danger is that most of us are looking for loopholes so we don't have to do the hard work of maintaining the unity in the body of Christ. We are not trying to provide such loopholes in this chapter.

We Should Not Divide Unless We Have Made Every Effort to Preserve Unity

We need to remember that the world is watching the way we treat each other. The people outside the church will not be interested in the message of the church if the church is a contentious place. Jesus told us that the world would know that we are His disciples if we have love toward each other. If we don't love each other, the world will turn away from their hope of salvation.

Second, we must remember that God hates it when His children fight. If you are a parent, you know how much it hurts you to see your children fighting. It doesn't hurt simply because it is annoying, it hurts because we want our children to be best friends. We want our children to have their siblings as someone they can play with, lean on, and turn to. Life is often hard and it helps to make the journey with someone who loves you. When members of the family fight, the Lord grieves. Jesus told us that the goal of our unity is to experience a joy similar to that of the Father and the Son.

We have an obligation to the Lord to pursue unity. God

shows us clearly that we are to seek reconciliation with our brothers and sisters in Christ. When we simply pack our bags and leave a church or a family, we are failing to fulfill our responsibility before the Lord. When we simply "walk away" we are short-circuiting our own spiritual growth. Much of the time we believe walking away from a conflict situation is sinful behavior. It is a way of avoiding our responsibility before the Lord.

The Example Of Jesus

Our precious Lord and Savior embodied the concept of love. He showed compassion to the hurting, forgiveness to the broken, and saw value in the rejected people of the world. Our goal is always to follow the example of Christ.

We must also point to the other side of Jesus. He called the Pharisees and Sadducees a "brood of vipers" and pronounced a series of "woes" on them (Matthew 23). These religious leaders were not fans of Jesus, and it seems the feeling may have been mutual. Jesus shows us that true love sometimes requires confrontation.

In John 2 and Matthew 21, there are records of Jesus creating quite a mess in the temple. Most likely these are two separate occasions, one at the beginning of His ministry, one during the last week of His earthly life. Matthew said Jesus, "overturned the tables of the money changers and the benches of those selling doves. [21:12]; In John we are told, "he made a whip out of cords, and drove all from the temple area, both sheep and cattle; he scattered the coins of the money changers and overturned their tables. To those who sold doves he said, "Get these out of here! How dare you turn my Father's house into a market!" [2:15,16]

There are other times when Jesus appears frustrated (as with the disciples, or the crowds who only wanted to see miracles) but these are really the only times we see Jesus in a contentious mood at all. What should we learn from His example?

First, notice that there is no record that Jesus ever became angry because of some *personal* offense. His anger was reserved for offenses against God or against someone else. He was angry with those in the temple because this holy place of worship had been turned into a marketplace. The holy had become profane. Jesus was angry with the Jewish leaders because they had distorted the message of salvation. They had perverted the gospel with their rules. He was angry because they were manipulating people through their long list of burdensome rules.

On the other hand when Jesus was personally attacked, he stood in silence or sought to make the encounter an opportunity to teach about God. His focus was on the Father and not Himself. He was willing to endure whatever was necessary, even death on the cross, if it would bring honor to the Lord.

As we examine the life of the apostles, we notice the same thing. Peter, James, John, and Paul all defend themselves when they are before the tribunals, but they always did so with the intent of sharing the gospel message. Their concern was never to preserve their life, comfort, or preference. They were willing to endure all things for the sake of Christ.

In the Book of Philippians, Paul talked about those who were using his imprisonment to advance themselves. They were exploiting Paul's hardship. It was a horribly opportunistic act. Rather than become angry, Paul said he was grateful that the gospel was advancing in spite of what was said about him.

Do you find this a little disconcerting? We do. Can we be honest? Isn't it true that the majority of our conflicts, the majority of our anger, and the majority of our church squabbles are over personal and personality issues? Most of our conflict is over petty, personal and sinful matters.

Most of the time, the issue at the center of conflict has nothing to do with God's glory. It is unfortunate that we seem more concerned about position, power, and status than we do theology. A church can drift from key Christian beliefs without anyone ever raising a question. However, if the lead part in the play is given to someone other than our child, we may find ourselves upset for days. We don't question sinful practices, but we won't hesitate to speak up when someone has a cup of coffee on the new carpet or our pet project is not included in the expansion plans for the church. We aren't concerned if the mission budget is slashed unless the budget for donuts for our Bible Study is taken away!

Even as we search our own lives and hearts, we realize that our zeal is much more intense for the personal things, than for theological things. We are much more concerned with our position than we are passionate for the glory of the Lord. This is common among human beings and those in the church are no exception. Such feelings amount to putting ourselves first. In a word, it is idolatry. We are actually seeking first *my* kingdom rather than the Kingdom of God.

We have things turned around! We must stop looking for "loopholes" and examine our own hearts. The first question in any conflict situation must always be, "Is there something that needs to change in me?" Only after we have done an honest personal inventory can we consider the more radical step of division.

Having said all this, we believe there are times when severing a relationship with a church, denomination or even another believer may be the wise course. However, even in these situations, division should only come as a last resort.

When a Church Abandons the Faith

The Episcopal Church recently faced a major crisis. The leaders of the church decided that they would elevate a bold, practicing, and unrepentant homosexual to the post of bishop. As a result of this action many congregations left the denomination and many people abandoned the Episcopalian church altogether. Were they right in doing so? We think they were.

The issue really has little to do with the bishop as an individual. The issue is the basis of authority for the church. The Bible clearly names homosexuality as a sin. It is affirmed in the Old Testament and reaffirmed in the New Testament (thus showing it is not merely a cultural command as some Old Testament commands may be). By ignoring the clear teaching of Scripture, the leaders of the Episcopal Church were overruling God's authority! We call this heresy. When a church departs from Scriptural authority, it is no longer the church; it is but a social institution.

Jesus cared about theology. We ought to care about it as well. There is a troubling trend in American Christianity. People tend to conclude that anything that draws a crowd must be evidence of God's blessing. That's a foolish conclusion. The circus, rodeo, and Major League baseball all draw crowds but that doesn't mean God is pleased with these things. When the Christians were being cast to the lions in the coliseums of Rome, crowds gathered and cheered. That did not make the event worship. The criteria of sound theology must never be, "but look at the crowd!" Our first question must always be, "is this Biblical?" When sound theology is abandoned a believer has to decide whether to stay and fight or simply leave the church.

When a Fight is Necessary

Up until this point, we have talked only about maintaining unity, but there are times when we must challenge the unity of our church. If a church is united under something other than the Word of God, it is not really a church anymore. We are called to work in restoring the church. Philippians 1:27 says,

> Whatever happens, conduct yourselves in a manner worthy of the gospel of Christ. Then, whether I come and see you or only hear about you in my absence, I will know that you stand firm in one spirit, contending as one man for the faith of the gospel.

Paul tells us that *whatever* happens, it is our job to make sure that our churches remain true to the Lord. We are to be unified as Christians, contending for the faith of the gospel. The word "contend" literally means to fight. We are to be united, but we are to be united in the "faith of the gospel." When the key points of the gospel are undermined or abandoned by a church, we must bring these facts to light. Many times, we will find that this action will upset people in the church, but Paul tells us that the only "manner worthy of the gospel of Christ" is to stand up for and fight for what is true.

In Jude 3, we see a nearly identical command. "Dear friends, although I was very eager to write to you about the salvation we share, I felt I had to write and urge you to contend for the faith that was once for all entrusted to the saints." Jude was writing to all Christians, saying that they must stand up for the faith they knew to be true. Every generation of Christians has people who try to sneak in and teach things other than the Word of God, and in every generation, Christians are commanded to fight against them.

The majority of us would see a problem in a church and instead of questioning the fidelity of what was being taught would simply leave. We're not sure that is the most loving thing to do. Many churches slide into heresy because no one dares to ask, "Where do we find this in the Bible?" or "Is that an accurate interpretation of what the Bible teaches?"

The question then is: if we are to fight, how are we to go about it? We think there are three steps in the process.

1. We need to find clear scriptural error
2. We need to bring that error to the leaders of the church
3. We need to bring that error to the members of the church

There are a number of essential Christian beliefs. If your church denies any of these there is a serious problem that needs to be addressed.

- The unique God/Man nature of Jesus (the deity of Christ). If your church denies that Jesus was the unique God/Man it is no longer a Christian Church.
- The Virgin birth of Jesus. Both Matthew and Luke clearly teach Mary was a virgin.
- Christ as the only way of salvation. If your church says there are many ways to Heaven, it has deserted the truth of the gospel.
- The Bible is the infallible authority for truth, faith, and living. If your church feels it can pick and choose from the Bible then it has abandoned Biblical authority and the faith. The Bible is either true in all its parts or it is not true at all.
- The necessity of a new birth. If your church denies that a person needs to be spiritually reborn to be "saved," they are denying the truth of John 3.
- The reality of heaven and hell. If your church does not believe in a real Heaven or Hell it is saying the Bible is not true and every other belief is open for negotiation. It has ceased to be a Christian community.
- The historical nature of the resurrection of Jesus. If your church does not believe in the literal resurrection of Jesus, it is no longer a Christian community. [5]

- The promise of a Second Coming. If your church denies that Christ is going to return (the timetable for such a return is an intramural debate), it has denied the clear words of Jesus and abandoned the true faith.

The Word of God amply supports all of these beliefs. If these truths are being denied you must do your homework. You must carefully search out the Scriptures and find clear teaching of these truths.

The Bible speaks clearly on many moral issues. You must find all the passages that talk about immorality, homosexuality, stealing, and other moral issues and examine these things carefully. We must only dare to fight when the Word of God is our foundation.

When Martin Luther stood before the Diet of Worms he was told to recant of his writings. Luther's response was appropriate. He said unless he was shown clearly by the Word of God that his teaching was in error, he could not and would not recant. Luther made himself subject to the authority of God's Word. So should we.

Second, we need to bring the error to the leaders of the church. Leaders are human beings. Sometimes we don't see what is obvious to others. Sometimes we think we know what the Bible says about an issue and never check it out ourselves. We must give the leaders the benefit of the doubt. We must not assume that they are intentionally leading the church away from sound teaching. (By the way, this is true for Pastors also. We need people to help us see problems we may not see.)

It is important that two things are present when talking to leaders. Paul tells us the Bible is useful for rebuking and correcting. (2 Timothy 3:16). The scripture should be our *only* basis for complaint. If you don't have a solid Scriptural basis for your complaint, the issue may very well be personal. If it is personal, all the steps listed previously about unity should be applied.

For example, if a church (or it's leaders) begins affirming that everyone will be saved in the end and no one will face Hell, you must show the leaders the Bible's teaching about judgment, Hell, and the verses that teach that only those who believe will be saved. On the other hand, if you believe your church has gone wrong because it is not singing the kinds of songs you think are most conducive to worship, you will have no clear Scriptural teaching to apply. In this later case you must decide whether it is an issue you can overlook out of love or whether you must quietly leave rather than be a source of contention in the body.

The second thing that needs to be present is love. John 15:12 says, "My command is this: Love each other as I have loved you." Jesus does not put up with sin, or with false teaching, He lovingly showed His disciples the error of their ways. Before we attempt to bring a scriptural error to our church leaders, we must spend time praying for our hearts to be made right. It is a good idea to also pray for a receptive heart in the one you will be talking to. Often *how* you say something is just as important as what you say. Seek God's wisdom.

Third, if the leaders of the church do not correct the error, we must alert the other members of our church to the error that exists. Throughout the New Testament, Jesus, Paul and John all tell the Christians around them when false teaching is occurring. Paul and John both wrote letters with the expressed purpose of combating false teachings that were pervading the church (Colossians and 1 John). In 2 Timothy 2:16-19, Paul actually names specific false teachers, and points out what aspect of their teaching is false. This is our last resort, but a step that needs to be taken if the leaders refuse to correct their error in teaching. We must still follow the same guidelines as before, have scripture and love at the forefront of our actions, but we must make the problem known to the members of the church.

Our intention is not to divide a church. We are not trying to cause trouble. What we are trying to do is keep those we love from drifting away from God into error. Our act is not a vicious act; it is an act of love.

On one visit to a church, there were no Bibles in the pews. The hymns lacked theological substance. The message was a secular and academic lecture that was similar to any lecture you might hear in a state University classroom. The sign out front said it was a "church" but it wasn't part of the body of Christ. There were people attending that church week after week blind to the fact that they were not truly Christian people. Someone needed to tell them.

On another day a group of ministers who were part of the fellowship of churches we belonged to had a meeting. In this meeting one of the Pastors confessed that he believed everyone went to Heaven in the end (that's called universalism). He felt his calling was to encourage everyone to love each other. Another Pastor (in the same meeting) thought the idea of a youth rally with a special speaker was a great idea, "as long as the speaker doesn't tell the kids Jesus is the only way to Heaven."

Let us remind you, this was a meeting of Pastors! This meeting was the beginning of a change of denominational affiliation for our congregation. In this case these Pastors were firmly convinced of their beliefs. The only course was for us to sever ties with these bodies. Was this a radical move? We don't think so. Paul said,

> Do not be yoked together with unbelievers. For what do righteousness and wickedness have in common? Or what fellowship can light have with darkness? What harmony is there between Christ and Belial? What does a believer have in common with an unbeliever? What agreement is there

between the temple of God and idols? For we are the temple of the living God. As God has said: "I will live with them and walk among them, and I will be their God, and they will be my people." "Therefore come out from them and be separate, says the Lord. Touch no unclean thing, and I will receive you." "I will be a Father to you, and you will be my sons and daughters, says the Lord Almighty." (2 Cor. 6:14-18)

The principle Paul gives us applies to all our alliances. If you are caught in a situation where the basic truth of the gospel is being denied, and you have discussed the issue unsuccessfully with those in authority, it is time to make a change.

Not every disagreement about Christian practice should be considered heresy. We've had people question our Christianity because: we didn't use the King James Bible; we didn't have an altar call; we weren't sure whether the rapture was going to be before the tribulation (we're not making this up); We've had people become angry about our understanding of the doctrine of predestination and the way we handle baptism. Most of these issues are issues the Church has disagreed on for centuries. You can find great Christian leaders on each side of these debates. These things are intramural debates (they are within the body of Christ) not issues that determine whether or not you are a Christian. (In fact, some of you are reviewing the above list and have determined we might be heretics because of these beliefs). As a believer, we should be able to fellowship with people who see things differently than we do in these areas. There is room for diversity in the body of Christ!

If your church or fellowship does not hold to Biblical Christianity it has ceased being a Christian church and it is probably time for you to push for change in your church or find a true Christian community to get involved in.

When Your Presence Hinders the Unity of the Church

We may need to leave a church when our presence is going to hamper the unity of the church. When there is an issue, hurt, or disagreement that you can't "let go of" then for your health and the health of the church, it is time to leave. If you have talked to those in leadership and worked with those who disagree with you but you cannot agree on an issue that you feel is essential, it is better to leave than stir up controversy.

There are too many churches where disgruntled members (often those who have ignored the Biblical guidelines for reconciliation) determine that they are going to stay in the church "no matter what." They become like a cancer on the congregation. They oppose every suggestion and keep an undercurrent of dissatisfaction churning by their talk. If you are one of those people, you need to leave the church for a simple reason: the unity of the church and the glory of God is more important than your attempt to "make a point."

Let's say one group of people in a church became convinced of the importance of speaking in tongues during worship. Since the rest of the church does not share this conviction, and these individuals are unwilling to restrain themselves for the sake of others, they should leave for the sake of the unity of the body.

Suppose your church hires a woman Pastor. You believe Scripture teaches that a woman should not be in that position. You discuss the relevant Biblical passages with those in leadership but your interpretation does not agree with theirs. If this issue is going to hinder your worship or make you feel that you are sinning, you should leave. If your conscience tells you something is wrong, you have an obligation to avoid that wrong.

Perhaps you are attending a church where you simply don't like the Pastor. You have tried to get to know the Pastor, you've invited him to dinner, gone into his office to visit, prayed for him and for your attitude toward him. However, his personality and yours are like gasoline and a lit match. You find it impossible to worship because every word he speaks is a distraction to you. Rather than slander the Pastor or push to have him replaced, it may be better to move on.

In each of these cases we must depart gracefully. We should not leave with anger. We must never slander our former church. We must simply agree to disagree.

There are times when we find ourselves saying, "Why should I leave, this was my church first?" We must keep in mind that it is Christ's church always. His glory is supreme, no matter how long we have attended or invested in the church. If staying in His church is going to bring dishonor to the Lord, we must leave.

When Growth Takes You in a Different Direction

We hesitate to mention this circumstance because of the potential for abuse. However, it needs to be listed. There are times when our needs require us to leave one group to be part of another.

We must combat the ever-present "consumer Christianity." This is when people hop from church to church until the novelty wears off and then move on. These people are always focused on "their needs." This approach to the life of community is destructive. We need long-term relationships to truly grow. Church membership involves giving as well as taking. We need to be around those who may view things differently than we do (it keeps us honest).

We must never be eager to leave our church. We may feel that "our needs aren't being met" when actually the real problem is our lack of involvement, our lack of spiritual discipline or our unwillingness to obey the Lord and do the hard work of reconciliation.

Having said all of this, there still may be a time when your own growth (or needs for growth) takes you in a different direction. Let's list some examples.

Perhaps you have been a member of a church for most of your life. You have been committed to this church and have worked to serve in any way possible. The church is small and struggling. It is only by sheer determination that the church keeps going. You love the people but there is little spiritual growth in your life and almost none in the life of your children (since they are the only children in the church). The focus of the church is not on growing in Christ, it is focused on how to keep the doors open. What do you do?

Certainly, no church can turn around if everyone "abandons ship." At the same time, you want your children to have a solid foundation. What do you do? It may be time to move to a different church.

Perhaps your physical situation has deteriorated and your church is no longer accessible. Maybe your church has gone to a more "expressive" form of worship and you crave quiet times of reflection in worship (or the other way around). It may be that your job has changed and you need to worship at a non-traditional time. You may need to find another church.

When you choose to attend a different church to help meet your changing needs, it is important to keep in mind that just because your old church is not meeting your current needs doesn't mean it isn't meeting the needs of others.

Conclusion

When we become a part of a church family we make a covenant with each other. That covenant is like a marriage ceremony. We agree that we will work through the hard times and enjoy the times of blessing. We agree to walk together knowing there will be tough times.

Sometimes a marriage ends in divorce. That situation is always tragic. Likewise, there are some times when a church relationship must end. It is always a sad time and should never be done without prayerful struggle.

Our hope is that even in these difficult times we can act for the right reasons and with the right attitude. We pray that even in our parting the world may see the grace of God in our behavior. May God grant that our partings be few.

Discussion Questions

1. Do you agree with the conclusion that Jesus and the disciples fought for principle while being unconcerned about personal offense? If so, do you agree that it is just the opposite for most people today? Give some concrete examples if you can.
2. What theological issues would you add to the "essentials" list? What theological issues would you remove?
3. What is the difference between heretical disputes and intramural disputes? Give some examples of each. Have you ever been involved in a church that had "abandoned the faith?" How did you handle the situation? Do you wish you had handled it differently?
4. Have you ever had an experience where you left a church because you would create division if you stayed?
5. Do you agree that people often leave a church for the wrong reasons? What would some of those reasons be?
6. Can you think of additional circumstances in which you might need to part company with a church family or another believer?

Chapter 9

Questions

Though we have tried to be thorough in this short book, we understand that there are still a host of questions on how to get along with others. In this chapter we address three common and difficult conflict situations.

What About the Person who doesn't want to be reconciled with me?

Paul told the Romans, "If it is possible, as far as it depends on you, live at peace with everyone." (Romans 12:18) As we've mentioned before, sometimes it is not possible to live at peace with everyone. Some people will hold on to a hurt forever. They seem to find solace in their misery. In some other relationships it seems that no matter what we do, the other person is going to take offense.

In this situation there are a couple of principles. First, *you* must do what God has told you to do. You need to make an effort at reconciliation. You must acknowledge your wrong and seek forgiveness. You must pray that God will change your heart and mend this relationship. You must not hold a grudge or you have not truly forgiven your brother from the heart. If we "write a person off" before we have made a serious attempt to be reconciled, we sin.

Second, you must make the situation a matter of prayer. Sometimes we are in situations where we have to continue to deal with a person on a daily basis. In these times we especially need to pray about *our* attitude. We cannot change the other person; we can only work at aligning our attitude with the attitude of Christ. We also need to pray *for* the other person. We must work at asking God to help us see the treasure that He sees in that person. We need to pray for that person to find the peace of God in his or her own life. As we learn to pray for others, God will help us see them with His eyes.

Third, if you have done what you are supposed to do, and the other person refuses reconciliation then it is time for you to be as "shrewd as snakes and innocent as doves." (Matthew 10:16). There are some people from whom we must keep our distance. We do this out of a desire for peace. Jesus told the disciples that when they entered a town and were not welcomed, they were to shake the dust off their feet and move on. (Luke 9:5) Sometimes we must do our best and then move on. In such situations you have fulfilled your responsibility before the Lord.

What if the difficult person is a family member?

When you have a difficult family member (a parent or sibling who abused you, an addict who takes advantage of people, a person you cannot please, someone who always has to be right) here are some guidelines.

First, never put yourself or others in a situation where you or they are in danger of abuse. If this tension is a result of an abusive relationship you need to be careful. The person needs to be prayed for but doesn't have to be invited to your home. If the person takes advantage of you financially, stop giving them money. With a friend or family member (don't do this alone) the abuse will need to be confronted before there is any hope of a reconciled relationship. Some people use the phone while others write a letter. It is important that you think clearly about what you want to say. In physically or sexually abusive situations, you need to talk to a counselor.

Second, always ask "Why is this person so difficult?" Much of the time a person is obnoxious because of his or her own insecurity. Some people just want to be loved and they don't know how to express that need. Others really are just trying to be helpful but aren't very good at it. Their approach may be wrong, but their heart may be right. If we can understand the heart of a person we can often learn to love that person in spite of what he or she does that annoys us.

Third, avoid situations that may lead to conflict. There is nothing wrong with simply saying, "I really don't want to talk about politics." If you refuse to take the bait, the conflict will not continue. We get into trouble when we start "looking for a fight." You don't have to respond to every sharp word or misstatement of another. We don't have to take everything as a personal attack. As we've mentioned earlier, some things you must just overlook in love. Sometimes we do have to say, "That's just the way they are." We can accept that fact or we can be miserable. If you look for a fight you will most likely be able to find one. It is up to you to refuse to add fuel to a conflict.

What about special circumstances?

Sometimes believers find themselves in circumstances that are extremely difficult. We want to honor the Lord, but

Difficult People

we also feel the need to stand up against those who would take advantage of us. We want unity, but we also feel the need to right a wrong. We want to glorify God, but we feel "giving in" will only perpetuate sin in another. What are we to do? Here are some practical examples.

A husband and wife get a divorce. In the process there is a custody fight. You have had primary care of the children but now your spouse is petitioning for sole or joint custody. What do you do? Do you tell the court about the negligence and inconsistency of your spouse? Do you fight or do you fold? What is the Christian thing to do?

Your spouse commits adultery. You try to forgive, but it happens again. Trust is destroyed. Your spouse tells you that he or she has never loved you. You don't believe in divorce, but you are beaten down. You have gone to counseling but it only seems to help for a while. Do you file for divorce, or do you risk more unfaithfulness? If you do feel it is time to separate, do you ask for spousal support or simply give your spouse everything and be free? What is the Christian thing to do?

You buy a new home. When you move into the home you find that there are major problems that were not revealed by the seller and the realtor. You request the items to be fixed but you are told, "All sales are final." What do you do? Do you take the seller (and we'll say the person is a fellow believer) to court?

You believe someone molested your child. Do you confront the person and extend forgiveness if he/she asks you to forgive their behavior, or do you call the police?

You see a fellow church member stagger out of a bar and get into their car. You see him weaving all over the road. You know that if he is pulled over for driving under the influence one more time, he will lose his license and it will make it very difficult for him to go to his job. Do you report him to the police or ignore the situation and hope nothing happens vowing to talk to him when he is sober?

A member of the church agrees to serve on committees and to do many things. However, many of these things are not completed and it is causing a problem. This member is sporadic in her attendance at meetings. The church decides to replace her on the board when her term is up but she asks to stay on the committee vowing that she will "do better."

You believe a law proposed by the City Council is immoral and wrong. Do you speak up, write letters, and engage in protests, or do you make it a matter of prayer and "stay out of it?"

It's quite possible that as you read the scenarios you answer, "It depends." There are some principles that we find in Scripture:

> Try to settle matters without going to court even if it means asking the church to serve as arbitrator. (1 Corinthians 6)
>
> It is better to confront a friend with their error than pretend everything is fine (Proverbs 27:6; Psalm 141:5)
>
> We are to seek good and not harm (Galatians 6:10)
>
> We should help each other overcome sin (Galatians 6:1,2)

Unfortunately, these principles are difficult to apply in the situations we've just listed. Some situations are not easy because there are so many variables. We believe there are principles that can help you decide what is best.

First, you need to accept the fact that your judgment is clouded. When you are in a conflict that is deeply personal and painful, it is difficult to think straight. You must be very careful! Since your judgment is clouded, beware of any rash actions. Most domestic crimes happen because people with clouded judgment do things they would never dream of doing if they were thinking clearly.

Since your judgment is clouded, seek some wise counsel. After you have searched the Scriptures, talk through the issue with a Pastor or respected and grounded Christian friend. It is always important to consider the consequences on all sides of the issue.

Whenever someone comes to us and tells us a story that has led that person to consider divorce, we urge counseling. Our first instinct must always be to save our marriage. However, depending on the situation, we may also encourage a person to talk to an attorney. By doing so, we are not encouraging divorce, we are encouraging the person to be well informed before they make any hasty decisions.

Second, you must decide if you are pursuing what is right or trying to exact revenge. When we are wronged, our first response is always to hurt someone as that person has hurt us (or hurt that person worse). We want to strike out and make the person "pay." Even in the case of the person driving drunk, we may see this situation as our opportunity to capitalize on the weakness of another. As believers we must always repent of such an attitude. Paul said,

Be kind and compassionate to one another, forgiving each other, just as in Christ God forgave you. Be imitators of God, therefore, as dearly loved children and live a life of love, just as Christ loved us and gave himself up for us as a fragrant offering and sacrifice to God. [Eph. 4:32-5:2]

Most people don't like this verse because they think it means we must always avoid any kind of conflict. That is not necessarily the case. Let's take some of our examples and show you why it might be loving to stand up for what is right.

In a custody battle the most loving thing for your children may be to make sure that the non-custodial parent provides for your children and keeps his/her promises. You do this not to "stick it to your ex-partner" but to get support for your children that will result in a good relationship with their non-custodial parent.

In a divorce situation sometimes the most loving thing you might do for an offending spouse is help him/her realize that there are consequences for their actions (such as an equitable division of assets). If we continue to allow a person to live with no thought for anyone other than himself, we are not helping that person at all.

In an unfair business dealing it may be most loving to show a brother that their business ethic is harming their testimony and force that person to live up to their word.

The most loving thing for our child would be to take steps to protect him or her from future abuse. It may take legal action to show your child that you believe what happened to him or her was wrong.

The best thing to do for the drunk driver would be to call the police to keep that person from hurting himself further or from hurting someone else. He may lose his license, but that is a consequence resulting from his choice, not yours.

A person in leadership may need to come to terms with the responsibilities of that leadership by being demoted until they can prove they will fulfill their obligations.

A spouse who is suffering abuse needs to leave the household or get their spouse to leave in the hope the abuser will "wake up" and get the help he or she needs. Leaving in this case doesn't necessarily mean you are getting a divorce. By leaving you are declaring that this kind of abusive relationship is not acceptable. [6]

If we care about our country we need to draw attention to unjust laws. Sometimes this may demand civil disobedience (when we deliberately refuse to obey an unjust law without engaging in any violence and with a full willingness to accept the consequences of our behavior.) We do this in the hope of awakening the consciences of others.

Do you get the idea? The most loving thing is not always to be passive. Sometimes you have to take a stand because it is the only way to change what is wrong. Sometimes you have to take a difficult and hard stand to help another person (the tough love approach). Remember, Paul advised the Corinthians to excommunicate the man who was engaged in a sexual relationship with his stepmother. (1 Cor. 5) It was not an act of narrow-mindedness; it was an act of love. By taking a firm stand, Paul hoped the man would wake up to his sin and repent.

We must be very careful. We are always prone to attribute the best motives to ourselves. We will always assume that we are championing the cause of truth, justice and the American way, but we may simply be trying to punish a person who hurt us. You must take time to pray and look at the situation, and your heart carefully.

Third, you must always maintain your Christian character. In a personal conflict situation like those we mentioned it is easy to lose your Christian character. In these tense times we must continue to be calm, kind (even if we have to be firm), and Christlike. Jesus at times was direct and even angry . . . but He always maintained His character.

If you find yourself sinking to name-calling, profanity, raising your voice or other abusive behavior, you are wrong. It is better to hang up on a phone call than let it become a shouting match. It is better to walk away than to attack. You must be clear on what you are trying to accomplish and focus on the godly end rather than the person who seems to be fighting that goal.

Christians often forget their Christian character when it comes to political and moral public debates. These public issues are the times when we most need to maintain our Christian character! The Lord's reputation is tarnished when

His children appear to be mean and vindictive.

Once I [Bruce] had an experience where a person had publicly attacked me for something of which I was innocent. I was new to a committee at a time when they were considering a controversial issue and for some reason this person decided that I should be the focal point of attack (perhaps because I seemed to be the weakest link). The person called me one day at my office and began to loudly rant and rave. I informed him that I would be happy to discuss things but I wasn't going to be yelled at. He continued to yell. I hung up. Ten minutes later (as I expected) the person showed up at my office and said, "Something happened and we were cut off." I responded, "No, I hung up!" My directness caught the person off guard. He asked, "Why would you hang up on me?" My response was simple, "I told you I would discuss things, but I would not argue about them." What followed was an adult discussion that was profitable and productive.

There are times when you may have to take a firm stand. These times are never easy and there will always be people who encourage you to "just forget it, give in and be done with it!" or "Don't get involved!" These people are not seeing the big picture. They are looking for what will ease tensions for them immediately. We need to be willing to consider what is best for the other person. To do what is easy is like ignoring cancer! It may be easier but that course can be deadly.

We must remember that even in these tough situations we still represent our Lord Jesus Christ. If we continue to show respect and integrity in our dealings with each other, God will do the rest. What if God has allowed us to face these things so we could glorify Him by the way we respond to the situation?

Conclusions

Suppose a woman is walking down the street in front of you on a winter day. As she walks along she hits a patch of ice and falls hard to the ground. Immediately you have a choice. You can run up and help her knowing that if she is injured you will be delayed waiting for help; or you can duck down an alley or cross to the other side of the street and pretend you saw nothing.

Which is easier? Obviously avoiding the situation is easier for *you*. Which is better? Helping another person is always better. In the same way, many of the issues we've raised in this chapter have an easy answer (avoid the issue) or a better answer (work to bring real help and healing even if it is through tough love).

There are no simple answers that can help you know what the right decision is in tough circumstances. The best thing to do is to prayerfully apply the Biblical principles in the desire to get along with others.

Discussion Questions

1. What other questions would you like to have answered?
2. Which of these questions do you think is the most common? What further suggestions would you add?
3. What other special circumstances can you think of that would fall under the category of special circumstances? Consider some of the following
    a. Medical malpractice (when do you sue and when do you forgive?)
    b. A person who is constantly asking for "more time" in paying their bill.
    c. Family estate issues
    d. Union Labor Strikes

  e. A child who is stealing from the family to buy drugs
4. What are some indicators that your judgment is clouded? What are some of the extremes people go to under these circumstances?
5. What do you think are some indicators that "tough love" is necessary? How can you tell the difference between tough love and a desire to punish another person?
6. What attitudes and behaviors might reveal an attitude of revenge rather than a concern to help the other person?
7. What experience do you have with situations such as the ones mentioned in this chapter?

Chapter 10

A Final Life Principle

❦

If there is one piece of advice that could stave off the majority of church conflict and help us get along with each other, it would be the words of James 1:19, "Let everyone be quick to listen, slow to speak, and slow to become angry." Most of our conflicts with each other would never happen if we could keep from re-acting to what someone said or did. In those reactions we often speak before we have all the facts, and our words are often sharpened with anger.

All the principles we've talked about so far can be enhanced and reflected in these words of counsel from James. It's great advice and it is a worthy goal for us all.

Quick To Listen

Much of the conflict that plagues our churches begins because we misunderstand what someone else is saying. We miss a word, over-emphasize another word, or miss the facial expression (which often tells us the seriousness of

Difficult People

what is said). Sometimes we are so busy talking (or thinking about what we want to say next) that we stoke the fires of controversy when we should be trying to understand it.

We need to take time to listen. I [Rick] was once in a Bible study systematically studying the book of James. In preparation for the study of James 1:19 the leader decided to spend a week without talking unless he absolutely had to. He began the study of James 1:19 with a short paper titled, "What I Learned While I Was Quiet."

In his paper, he listed the different things he learned when he actually took time to let others speak. He discovered that many of the people he thought were people who "didn't say much" were actually quiet because no one gave him or her a chance to speak! When the leader was quiet he discovered that the quiet folks have some insightful and helpful things to say.

The leader learned that often he drew an erroneous conclusion about what someone was saying because he interrupted them before they had a chance to finish. When he took the time to listen he found that he reached an entirely different conclusion than if he had interrupted (which he often did). He was humbled by the fact that people thought something must be wrong because he was quiet and listened to them and didn't interject his own thoughts.

When we take the time to listen to other people, we can learn many things. We will hear details that are vital to the conversation. If we listen, we may find that the words that we took offense to were words that meant something different than what we initially thought. We may have been insulted when someone was just giving us a playful hard time. We may have concluded that someone was being critical when they were actually very positive and trying to help us be even better (speakers are especially sensitive here).

I [Bruce] have a man who "rates" every one of my sermons like an Olympic judge. When he leaves the church he puts a card in my pocket that has a score, such as "9.8," along with an explanation of the score. Some people think this is offensive to me. It's not. I understand that the man is simply giving me feedback. If I listen I can learn important things that will help me be a better speaker. His words are almost always very encouraging.

When we take time to listen and hear, we demonstrate to another person that we value him. The most precious gift we can give is our attention! Listening says, "What you have to say is important to me. Your contribution, insights, and knowledge are something I want to hear." Everyone appreciates a person who will listen.

When we listen with our eyes as well as our ears, we gain important information. If we are paying attention, we may see that tear in the eye of another. We may notice the clenched fist or the reddened face. We may see the look of hurt, or the look of eager anticipation to share and contribute. You can hear a great deal if you listen with your ears and your eyes.

If we can learn to listen we will grow spiritually. Someone has said, "it's not how much of the Bible you get through that matters; what matters is how much of the Bible gets through you!" In order for the Bible to get through us, we need to take time to meditate (purposeful listening). We must listen to the words of God's Word and also listen for the "still small voice" of God's Spirit as He applies those words in our lives.

Here's a suggestion for you: why not deliberately plan a day of silence. Make it a point to pay attention. Ask questions only and see what you can learn from others. Listen to others and try to understand their hearts as well as their words. In addition to reading God's Word really work at listening to the part that you read. Read it in several versions until you understand what God is saying. Let His word sink into your heart so that it will be able to express itself through your hands and feet. It is better to read less and understand more than it is to read much without understanding.

We need to work hard to make sure we hear correctly. It is easy to draw the wrong conclusions from what someone says. For example, someone says, "You look nice!" What does that mean? Does it mean, "You don't look great, but you look nice" or "You look nice for a change" or "You look wonderful!"

Suppose your church is embarking on a building program. The building committee presents the plan to the governing board or congregation and asks for comments. One man from the church stands up and says, "I don't like the plan." Immediately the building committee often will get defensive.

If you respond to this man immediately, there is a good chance that you are going to overreact. You may quickly conclude that this man is an obstructionist. You find yourself angry that this man is "standing in the way of God's will." However, if you respond to the man by saying, "What don't you like about the plan?" He might respond in several ways:

- I don't like the whole idea of a building program because I don't think we need the plan.
- There is a part of the plan that I don't like. I don't think the fellowship hall is big enough.
- I don't like the plan because I think it is going to take too long. We need to get started on the building sooner than your plan recommends.
- I don't like the plan because I think there is a better way to raise the money.
- I don't like the plan because I don't think the church can handle that much debt.

Once you have listened well enough to understand what the man's statement means, you now have a more focused criticism to deal with. By taking the time to listen and to clarify what a person is trying to say, you gain understanding. Understanding will always diminish conflict. This man is more likely to support whatever plan the church adopts if he feels his ideas and thoughts have been fairly heard. Besides, the man may have a point!

A good rule of thumb is this: ALWAYS clarify. It's always a good idea to check to see if what you think you understand is really the correct message. You can do this by simply asking, "Do I understand that you are saying _____ (you like the way I look; you are in favor of the building plan; you think I talked longer than necessary)." Clarifying will eliminate misunderstanding and will enhance growth.

Slow To Speak

Have you ever said something stupid? (Yes, that in itself is a stupid question!) Perhaps you see a man in the mall parking lot with a hanger down the side of his car window, and you ask, "Did you lock your keys in the car?" Perhaps you've asked the woman in the wedding dress and the man in the tuxedo, "Did you just get married?" There are times when we know we said something dumb as soon as the words leave our mouth. People are right in answering us, "Duh!"

Unfortunately, some of the dumb things we say can hurt people. How many children have been wounded because of a thoughtless word from a parent? How many spouses have been humiliated by a story shared in public by their mate? How many parents have had their heart broken by the hateful words of a child? How many people have been hurt because a secret was thoughtlessly shared with someone else? How many people have left a church because of a thoughtless word? How many people have been pushed away from the Savior because of a negative comment from one of His children?

It is clear that James had a very practical reason for us to be slow to speak. When we speak quickly, we speak out of reflex and often say things that we would choose to take back if we had the chance. Rather than regretting what we say, we need to choose our words carefully. This axiom is easy to say, but difficult to put into practice. Here are some suggestions that might help us all.

First, we need to pay attention to the order of the suggestions given by James. If we are quick to listen and wait for a person to finish speaking before we begin to speak, we will avoid many problems. If we listen and process what we are hearing BEFORE we start to speak, we will be less likely to respond inappropriately.

We must stop being afraid of silence! It is o.k. to have a little silence in a conversation as a person ponders what another has said. Solomon says, "When words are many, sin is not absent. He who holds his tongue is wise." (Proverbs 10:19) Why do we feel that we need to comment on every situation? Why do we feel we need to immediately respond to what another says? Why do we feel the need to over-elaborate on every issue? You will get in less trouble by what you say if you say less. Give others a chance to talk; you will be surprised at what you learn.

We are always surprised by teachers who ask a question of the class and then when no one answers immediately, they give the answer! Is it possible the class is shy? Could the students be thinking? Why not let silence do its work?

A second way we can facilitate being slow to speak is to actually slow the cadence of our speech. In other words, we can actually speak more slowly. Too often we say things before we even realize what we are saying. If we speak more slowly we will have more time to weigh our words. Sure, you can take this too far. You can talk so slowly that people forget what you were talking about before you finish talking! Most of us could slow down greatly and never risk talking too slow.

It is obvious how important this is for keeping the peace in the church. Our tendency in times of crisis is to talk fast (so we can get everything out we want to say before someone interrupts us) and we speak carelessly. Sometimes we say things we didn't mean and didn't think through before we let them fly. If we speak more slowly we will give ourselves a chance to hear what we ourselves are saying!

Third, we can speak softly. In a conflict situation the volume of the conversation often rises rapidly. If you allow yourself to keep raising the volume of your conversation not only will others hear the dumb things you say, but also it will be less likely that anything good will come from the conversation. When two people are yelling at each other it is difficult, if not impossible, to actually hear what another is saying. If you want to communicate, it is better to speak softly so people have to concentrate to hear you.

Slow To Anger

If we exhibit the first two characteristics, it will make this third one much easier. If we are quick to speak, we will become extremely angry, and our anger may grow very rapidly. If we don't listen, it is easy to think someone is attacking us when they really aren't. Following the principles of being quick to listen and slow to speak will help us to be slow to become angry.

Sometimes, even when we do understand what a person is saying (because we have listened), anger may still rise within us. Before we allow anger to progress too far, we need to ask ourselves why we are becoming angry. More often than not, it is because of our own sinful pride. We are being selfish, and that is why we are angry. When we ask ourselves what is causing us to become angry and our responses are full of words like, I, me, my, and so forth it may be a sign that our problem is selfish pride.

Before we speak in anger we need to go back and evaluate why we are angry as we suggest in chapter three. Most of the time our anger is a result of our embarrassment (which we seek to cover with hostility); fear (which causes us to lash out at another); frustration (that we take out on someone) or hurt. If we can identify the actual reason for our anger, we will often be able to address those "real" issues rather than being hateful and destructive.

The command given to us to be *slow* to anger does not mean we should *never* be angry. There are times when we should be angry. We should be angry when there is a wrong being committed, or when people are dishonoring God. Jesus was angry with those in the temple because they were making a mockery of the place of worship. We should hope that our holy passion would make us angry in a similar circumstance.

Even in our anger we must continue to be quick to listen. Often the person who said something to make us angry may have already realized their error and will be trying to correct it. If we are not paying attention, we will only make the problem worse. If we listen, we can quickly resolve the issue and skip straight to the step of forgiveness.

The principle that dominates in all of these ideas is the principle of self-control. We must train ourselves to listen carefully, listen fully, speak deliberately, and keep our impulsive anger under control. We suggest you memorize this verse and post it in various locations that will help you remember this important and practical advise from James.

These principles from James chapter 1 seem so obvious that we tend to overlook them. When we examine them closely, we see that they are the very basis of almost every conflict situation. These truths underlie all of the steps that have been laid out elsewhere in this book. Every conflict situation can be handled in two ways: our way or God's way. We hope that it is clear throughout the course of this book what God's way is.

In the introduction to the book, we asked the simple question, as the world looks at the church today, does it see Jesus? Our answer to that question was that instead of seeing Jesus the world often sees bitterness, anger, and selfishness. The church has lost its distinctiveness because it handles disagreement just like the rest of the world. As Christians, we are called to love one another and to reflect the light of Christ to a world shrouded in darkness. The best way to do that is to live a life of community in our churches that is markedly different from the world.

We encourage you to take the concepts in this book and apply them to your life. Share what you learn with others. If we do that, the church will once again begin to shine like the light it was meant to be. May God help us to once again be set apart by the love that is evidence of the Lord working in and through us. May the world notice our love, not so that they may be drawn to us, but so they may be drawn to the One who has loved them since the creation of the world.

May God help us to get along with each other. Not just for our sake, but also for His.

Discussion Questions

1. Of the three commands in James 1:19, which do you think is the most difficult to do?
2. Why do you think we have such a difficult time listening?
3. Define "listening."
4. Why do you think some people are "talkers" and some are not? How can a talker learn to give others a chance to speak?

5. Do you agree that almost all anger is caused by embarrassment, anger, frustration or hurt? Can you think of any other causes of anger?
6. Identify the cause and discuss the right way to respond to these situations
    a. A person cuts you off in traffic
    b. Your spouse suggests you are not holding up your part of the relationship.
    c. Someone notices you have toilet paper stuck to your shoe.
    d. You are making repairs in the kitchen (which you aren't enjoying) and you hit your thumb with a hammer
    e. Someone is critical of your leadership of a meeting

Endnotes

1. Early Church Fathers- Ante-Nicene. Volume 3 chapter 39 by Tertullian in Apology
2. Dallas Willard SPIRIT OF THE DISCIPLINES (San Francisco; Harper, 1990) p. 259
3. www.hispeace.org is an excellent site with many additional resources such as this. This is adapted from THE PEACEMAKER: a BIBLICAL GUIDE TO RESOLVING PERSONAL CONFLICT Copyright 1997 by Ken Sande.
4. Some good books are FIRESTORM by Jerald Susek , THE PEACEMAKER by Ken Sande and LEADING YOUR CHURCH THROUGH CONFLICT AND RECONCILIATION (Christianity Today/Leadership 1997);
5. See Bruce's book FINDING YOUR WAY THROUGH THE FOG chapter two for a more thorough illustration of this problem.
6. For people in this situation we recommend Dr. James Dobson's Book LOVE MUST BE TOUGH

CPSIA information can be obtained at www.ICGtesting.com
Printed in the USA
LVOW07s0000120115

422385LV00001B/191/P

9 781597 810647